The Seasons Within

Leon Davis

Budgie Press Pty Limited

The Seasons Within

Author: Leon Davis

In accordance with the Copyright Act 1968 a copy of each printed book published must be lodged with the National Library. Under relevant State or Territory Legislation a copy must also be lodged with the appropriate library or libraries in the state of publication.

National Library of Australia Cataloguing-in-Publication entry

Author: Davis, Leon, 1952.
Title: The Seasons Within / Leon Davis.
Edition: 1st edition.
ISBN: 978-0-6489118-2-1 (pbk.)
Notes: Includes index.
Dewey Number: A823.4

Publisher: Budgie Press Pty Limited, ACN 129 875 878
              Published, 2008

Printed by: BookPal Australia
              www.bookpal.com.au

The Author

Leon Davis was born in Australia in 1952. He comes to writing after extensive studies in law and metaphysics.

In his younger years Leon was an avid sportsman competing at the elite level in swimming, athletics, rugby, basketball and, in his 40's in Ironman triathlon.

After becoming involved with health programs in the early 1980's, Leon was introduced to 'The Elements of Man' and other metaphysical understandings that have had a profound effect on him.

A single father of two teenage sons, he lives in Sydney where he operates a small legal practice.

DEDICATION

This story concerns Nature and the way it manifests in our lives through physical and emotional energy, our relationships and the environment.

This work is dedicated to those young persons who are capable of feeling the energy of Nature around them, of recognising the Life Force within themselves, and the way it influences our lives.

It is my hope that this work will stimulate in you many more questions than answers.

ACKNOWLEDGEMENT

The seed for this story was planted many years ago when I first experienced the magic and mystery of Queen's Park in Invercargill, New Zealand. It was germinated by the metaphysical understandings brought to me by T. Glynn Braddy who has been a student of the source material since it was delivered.

I wish to acknowledge an Old Chinese philosopher who brought to the 20th century the original source material that comprises what is now known as 'The Elements of Man'. The wisdom and metaphysics communicated in this book as the words of Old Chinese arrived through the mediumship of Marshall N. Lever.

The words of Old Chinese are reproduced here verbatim from tape recordings made in the mid 1970's. Though his language is sometimes a little contorted I feel that it is important for the reader to feel the energy of the exact dialogue. When Old Chinese uses the word "Peace" he means "Yes" or "Correct".

Leon Davis, 2008

TABLE OF CONTENTS

Prologue

After an exhausting day of travelling, my head lolled back. I was tired, hungry and needed to rest.

Suddenly, I jerked forward and, despite the frigid temperature, I could feel beads of sweat breaking out on my brow. Tears of grief and sadness unexpectedly welled in my eyes as a wave of nausea gripped the pit of my stomach. Gazing through the car window I saw nothing unusual, only the imposing gates of a park, yet I felt a disturbing presence.

I had no idea what was happening to me. I could not understand why I'd become so emotional as I sat in the back seat of a car beside two children. Taylor, eight, and Kristie, five, both stared at me in disbelief. I could see them wondering why this stranger from Sydney was sitting next to them crying. In the front seat, Carolyn and her husband sat unaware of my state.

We had just left the airport and they were driving me to their home. This was my first visit to New Zealand since I'd toured the North Island on a schoolboy rugby tour at age 17. Her family had never met me before and I had no idea where I was going.

Confused and embarrassed, the only thing I was certain of was the suffocating sense of foreboding that enveloped my body. I could feel death surround me and it felt like it was in some way connected to the park.

When we arrived at their home in Margaret Street I was still distressed and felt compelled to go outside to the open veranda to gather my thoughts. Carolyn and her family were dumbfounded by my actions, as the weather was close to freezing.

Outside, I reflected how in the early 1980's, without really being conscious of it, I had started my metaphysical quest. I'd become involved in a health program that was designed to improve my well-being and to reduce body dimensions and excess weight. Very quickly however, it became clear that the insights I was gaining from my teacher were the threshold to much deeper understandings.

Toward the end of one of those courses my teacher, T. Glynn Braddy had told me how, in the mid 1970's he had been involved in a series of lectures in London. The result was that he began a life-long journey with metaphysics. He later developed his own teachings that were based on a series of channeled lectures known in the 20th century as 'The Elements of Man'.

In the years to follow I was privileged to attend on many occasions the seminars that he evolved from the 'The Elements of Man' material—understandings that became another story, as did my own. Each time I left a teaching I felt imbued with a deeper understanding of life and how ancient principles could still have an impact upon our everyday existence, even in modern times.

During the 1980's I worked diligently with both the metaphysical understandings and the information I had received pertaining to my own spiritual evolution.

Through the early 1990's, without being conscious of it, my attention had partly shifted and much of my focus was directed to my sporting endeavours.

I recalled how, at 39 years of age, and feeling a little too old to play competitive basketball any longer, I'd decided to train as a triathlete. I acquired my first push-bike, trained hard, and competed in more than 20 short course races in my first year. By the end of my second year I was training for the Foster Ironman, one of Australia's most famous triathlon races, which consists of a 3.8km swim, a 180.2km bike ride and a 42.2km marathon.

Training for Ironman races, which included long rides and runs, gym sessions and swimming with a 5.00am swim squad, consumed many hours each week. Though somewhat of a deviation from metaphysics, the hours of training were beneficial to me in other ways and I learnt a lot about my inner spirit and drive. After completing five Ironman races, I'd had to quietly admit to myself that I was becoming somewhat dependent on the self-confidence that I gained from completing these races. The 'high' was addictive and I needed it to carry me through the following year.

Although it was not always apparent to me at the time, with hindsight I saw that I had still been 'on track' in my spiritual evolution.

And so, on Carolyn's cold veranda I reflected on how, in 1992 I'd become re-acquainted with this remarkable young woman with whom I had worked some years earlier. She lived in Invercargill, at the southernmost point of the South Island of New Zealand. It was at her invitation that I found myself here and without understanding why, reviewing my metaphysical journey.

I sat alone in the cold for many hours attempting to reconcile my feelings of impending death and trying to understand their source. All I knew was that there was some connection with the park.

I returned inside numb from the cold and confused.

Carolyn was still awake, but her family had all gone to bed. I recounted to her the feelings of impending death I'd experienced around the park. I also told her I felt, in some way, that her son Taylor was involved. Understandably she became concerned for him and questioned me on what I thought was happening. I could not offer her any rational explanation.

It was approximately 3.00am before I went to bed that night, feeling fearful and longing for understanding and with my questions still unresolved.

Suddenly my eyes jerked open. Or did they? Was I still asleep or had I been jolted to consciousness by the entity near the door? I could not tell if the figure was real or not, but I did recognise the Being I had feared meeting for so long.

I sensed that the figure was communicating with me and thought I heard it speak my name, "Leon", in a deep guttural voice. But perhaps I only felt it?

I knew that this was an energy associated with 'Quest' and the thing I feared most in my life—change. In my meditations I had been preparing myself for some major life changes for many months. Those changes related to the end of my marriage and the break-up of our family unit.

But now I was being called upon to take action. The energy of change itself had come to visit me in the form of a darkly shrouded and indistinct, yet frighteningly real figure. I could not see a face, but there was no mistaking that this energy was here to confront me with some kind of challenge.

It felt somehow unfair that this opportunity was presented

when I was not even certain that I was awake. Nevertheless, I knew that in this moment I was being given the opportunity to change my life in some profound way and that my decision must be immediate and unwavering.

Still uncertain of both my surroundings and my state of consciousness, the challenge was offered, wordlessly. I could choose to pass into a green meadow dotted with bright yellow and white flowers with the knowledge that safety resided there. The alternative was to immediately leap into a dark yawning cavern.

The fear in my body was palpable. I wanted to vomit but the immediacy of his demand required an instantaneous response. Somewhat numbed by my semi-conscious state, I knew what I must do in order to succeed.

I jumped and felt myself falling, tumbling, endlessly into the blackness to what I knew must be certain death—or worse—upon rocks at the base of what I imagined to be a gigantic chasm.

I woke suddenly in a cold sweat as the first streaks of dawn filtered into the icy room. My panic subsided slowly as the rising sun's warmth banished the darkness around me.

I knew in those moments of awakening that my life had changed forever. The messenger was gone but the lesson was not. I knew I had met the challenge and that my leap of faith had somehow emerged from a deep inner calling. I would never fear change again. From that point on my life would be a celebration of choice.

The next morning, to her eternal credit, Carolyn took me back to the park. As soon as I passed through those imposing gates, the now familiar feeling of foreboding again engulfed me.

Confused, my trembling legs carried me into the park, towards the place I had seen in my mind's eye the evening before. Or had it all been a mere figment of my imagination?

My feet hesitated near a silent stream that meandered around a tree-studded knoll. My attention was pulled to a small grassy area near the edge of the creek. I knew that death had been present here. But who and why remained a mystery.

I looked up to get my bearings. This place was adjacent to the boundary of the park and directly across the road from Invercargill Hospital.

I left the park that day even more confused, feeling emotional and consumed by irrational fears. Was I having some kind of premonition about a death that would occur at that place in the park or had I tripped into something from the past?

Though I had been in Invercargill for less than 24 hours it was time to go. Reluctantly my focus switched to making it to the airport in time to catch my plane home.

Seated adjacent to me on the international flight was a curious Frenchman who wanted to talk to me. Still in distress and unable to communicate with him, I sat with tears of sadness trickling down my cheeks, determined once and for all, to resolve this puzzle.

During the flight I remembered that I could use kinesiology or muscle testing, which I had learned as part of the health program, to establish what had occurred. To my absolute amazement both the questions and my body's responses to them came quickly and easily.

I discovered that my body held a memory from the year 1892. I had been the Harbour Master of the Port of Bluff near Invercargill. My wife in that lifetime had been my friend, Carolyn, though her body shape and dimensions were vastly different to those in this life.

A young girl of about 16 lived in my home with my wife, our children and myself. It seemed that the girl whom we had taken in as a favour to a friend, had fallen pregnant to a person who was unknown to us. The energy that I felt from the park was related to this girl's journey through the park towards the hospital. She did not make it to the hospital and died in childbirth, alone at that sombre place by the creek. Her baby had also died.

I sensed that the spirit of the baby who died with its mother that night was somehow close to me. My muscle testing indicated that this child's spirit had incarnated into the body of Carolyn's son, Taylor. This explained my feelings on the veranda and the close bond that had evolved between us in this life.

Following my return to Sydney, I telephoned Carolyn and shared with her what I had gleaned. Instead of dismissing it and laughing at me, she promptly went to the Museum at the Harbour Master's office in Bluff. There she easily accessed the appropriate records and through her research was able to ascertain that the Harbour Master in Bluff in 1892 was a Scotsman by the name of Norman McDonald. He had been born in Inverness, Scotland, had joined the Merchant Marine and sailed to Melbourne. Later he moved to Bluff where he was appointed Harbour Master in the late 1880's.

Carolyn's confirmation of the information my body held amazed me and I was flooded with understanding. When she mentioned his name and date of birth I was overcome with emotion and the certainty of 'knowing'. The final confirmation came when she produced copies of photographs of Norman McDonald. To my utter disbelief they bore a striking resemblance to me in this life.

On subsequent trips to Invercargill I re-visited the park and after some searching, again located the place where the events of that extraordinary night had occurred. It looked different to the place I'd originally seen in my mind's eye, as in the intervening years, a row of large trees had grown up, screening the location from view.

Now, years later, I was returning to Invercargill with my 13 year old son, Jonathon, for reasons that were not yet fully clear to me. All I knew was that I felt an irresistible pull to introduce Jonathon to the wonder and mystery of Queen's Park—and I knew enough to trust that.

Captain Norman Macdonald,
Bluff Harbour Master
1888 – 1911

Chapter 1 – The Beginning

The first snow of winter had left a light dusting of powder upon the trees and bushes in the park. Filtered through a sullen cover of clouds the sun's rays barely touched the almost frozen ground.

Jonathon surveyed the desolate scene and shivered uncontrollably. The park was silent and the only signs of life were the snowy footprints of a few tiny animals. Totally alone in this unfamiliar place he was swamped with dread at the thought of having to live here.

The same questions had consumed him since he arrived— Who am I? Where am I going? Why am I here in New Zealand?

Imperceptibly, a distant sound filtered into his consciousness. It was a rhythmic "boom, boom, boom." He tried to ignore it but it grew steadily louder. Turning around slowly he saw an indistinct figure sauntering towards him.

Jonathon glanced furtively towards the park gate. He felt tempted to run. However his father's words echoed inside his head and kept his feet rooted to the ground—"Never fear the unknown."

Reluctantly he turned to face the belligerent-looking figure ambling towards him. It dawned on him that the noise came from the rugby ball the boy was bouncing on the frozen grass. "Boom, boom, boom." The sound filled his head as the boy now strode confidently towards him. Jonathon was scared, but at the same time curious.

"Who are you?" the boy demanded.

"I'm Jono," he replied.

"So what are you doing here?"

"I...I just arrived in town yesterday and thought I would come and check out the park".

"I saw you at school today and wondered who you were. I'm Taylor. I live here and I know every inch of this park," he said confidently.

Jonathon eyed the teenager cautiously. Taylor was older than he was with a muscular build and a crop of blonde curly hair atop a confident and inquisitive face. Jonathon stuck out an unsteady hand and Taylor shook it.

Taylor continued sizing him up, observing Jonathon's strongly-built body, chiselled face and short dark hair. His city clothes were out of place here. Taylor was aware he was making the younger boy nervous and secretly enjoyed having the upper hand.

"So what brings you to this park?" demanded Taylor.

"Oh, my Dad told me that when you go to a new place you should check out the park. He says parks reflect the type of people who live in a town. I'm not sure I really know what he means. This place is pretty derelict isn't it?"

"Oh, I don't know about that," said Taylor. "This is a really neat place. There are things to do here all year round and there are some fantastic hidden parts."

Jonathon mumbled,

"Well, like, would you show me sometime?"

"Sure." said Taylor. "Do you play rugby? There are some really neat places to kick a ball here."

"Yeah, I played a year of rugby in Sydney before we came over here," said Jonathon.

Taylor looked at Jonathon and wondered why this Sydney boy had come to New Zealand. There was something strange yet intriguing that he did not understand about him. Though he did not know why, he suspected that there was more to Jonathon than met the eye.

"How about I show you around the park and introduce you to some of my mates at school?"

The two boys met in the park the next afternoon. Taylor showed Jonathon most of the easily accessible areas of the park and Jonathon quickly came to understand what the other boy saw in it. Even though the park looked empty, Jonathon could feel a strength and beauty lying dormant within it.

It was early winter and Jonathon rugged up to face his second week at school. Now that he had met Taylor, he didn't feel so lonely.

That afternoon as the boys wandered around the park they felt the silence and the absence of animals and birds. Taylor had done a little duck shooting the previous year and knew that ducks left their nesting grounds in winter.

He explained,

"The animals and birds know that winter has arrived but they'll come back as soon as the weather warms up."

Jonathon recalled the snowy footprints and suspected that the park was not as empty as it seemed.

One afternoon they stood with their backs resting against the base of an oak tree. Like most of the larger trees it had shed its leaves but they could still sense the life within, even though it looked dead on the outside.

Digging around the roots of a bush, the boys discovered a whole world of insect life.

Taylor said to Jonathon,

> "Look at these ants. They're scurrying about gathering food like there's no tomorrow!"

The animals and insects had not disappeared from the park at all but were simply doing what was needed to conserve body heat and food in preparation for the cold nights and days to come.

Not too far from the park entrance was a large body of water rimmed by icy sandstone flagging. Winter had left the duck pond, and the small creek that filled it, almost frozen and apparently devoid of life. Jonathon stared at it, wondering whether the dark, freezing water was as empty as it appeared.

Chapter 2 – Why?

That night Jonathon returned home looking bewildered. Concerned, I asked him what had happened, but initially Jonathan would say very little. Later, over dinner, I again questioned him.

> "Jono, how are you settling in?"

> "Dad, I still don't really understand why we're here. But it's not too bad. I've met a boy called Taylor who is showing me around Queen's Park. He grew up here and he knows it all."

I said,

> "Did you say Taylor?"

I stared at the floor recalling the metaphysical journey that Carolyn and I had undertaken over the years. Now I had returned to her home-town where I felt the park would be Jonathon's teacher. I understood that the teaching would be for Jonathon and not for her or me and so had not yet contacted her.

I did not hear Jonathon's response but knew his journey had commenced. I realised in that instant that it must be *his* journey. Any advice I offered would need to come from a spiritual place, rather than my role as his father.

Trying to sound casual I said,

> "That's great Jono. It's good to have someone to show you around."

Was I reassuring him—or perhaps myself? I sat quietly

reflecting on how the journey might potentially be confusing for a teenager, unconsciously rubbing my left shoulder which was a habit of mine.

For a few moments he sat quietly then put down his knife and fork, nodding at my shoulder.

"Dad, I've always wanted to ask you. How on earth did you ever finish that Ironman back then? You were trussed up like a turkey. You had a broken shoulder."

Looking at my son, I realised it was a reasonable question.

"It wasn't my shoulder. It was a dislocated acromioclavicular, or AC, joint."

I thought for quite a while before continuing.

"It's a long story Jono and I'm not sure I can even explain it in words. It had something to do with my preparation for the race. I used to think of each phase, including my preparation, as being connected to a season of the coming year.

And how I performed was like some unseen link to the future. In each race I was literally stepping into the unknown in a way that was shaping my future and that's what helped me to keep going—even though I was injured."

I pushed my plate a little further away, gazing in the direction of the wall where my mind was running an invisible movie and re-living the crash. It had happened just two weeks before the Ironman race and I could still feel the impact of my shoulder hitting the road. As I disentangled myself from the fallen bikes and riders I

14

knew I was injured but my first thought was for the race—even as I rode with one arm to the hospital.

"Jonathon, you've done a couple of short triathlons. They were hard for you but you finished. It's just like life. We never start something we can't finish. Your spirit, which is the essence of your soul, will always provide the power for your body and your mind to succeed in any endeavour that you undertake. It is simply a matter of giving it your best."

"But Dad, we're talking about a race. Does it really matter whether you even compete, let alone finish or win?" Jonathon said, forgetting about his food.

"Jono, there's no easy answer to that. For me, competing in an Ironman is not about winning or losing. It's about learning how I cope with challenges. For someone else that answer might be different. If we listen very carefully to the clues that the Universe gives us and ignore the criticism of others we'll always make the right decisions and do what's right for us."

I reflected for a few moments on the journey now facing Jonathon and honed my words with this in mind.

"I used to prepare for a race by thinking about it as being like the four seasons in a coming year of my life.

My preparation was like the winter. That was the hardest part. It's all about understanding your inner drivers and having a vision for yourself. The swim is like springtime—the deep water is like your emotions. The ride is summer. You feel the breeze in your face and you need to think and be strategic. The

15

run is like autumn. Your feet are pounding the earth and it's really physical and as you near the end you're preparing to celebrate! And no sooner do you finish than you're preparing for the next one.

Do you understand what I am saying?"

Jonathon looked at me, then at his food and then at the wall.

"Sort of," he said slowly, "I'll think about it."

Chapter 3 – The Meeting

The next day Jonathon went to the park alone. He still felt a little overwhelmed by the events of the past few weeks and said he wanted to go to the park, just to think. He'd made a new friend and learned that real warmth did exist here, despite the cold that stifled the landscape.

Later he stood near the park entrance for several long minutes seeking some glimmer of warmth. As the gloomy, dim landscape seeped into his consciousness he began to sense that someone was watching him. Unnerved, he slowly turned in every direction but could not immediately see what it was he was sensing.

Then, through the heavy, mist-laden air, a sliver of reflected light caught his attention. A ghostly figure, draped in silvery robes, was seated on a park bench almost imperceptible against the snowy landscape dotted with leafless trees.

Although the figure was some distance from him he knew the hand was beckoning to him. Again Jonathon looked in every direction to see if the figure could be motioning to someone else but there was no-one in sight. Still, for some reason, he placed a finger to his chest as if to enquire whether it was him that the figure was addressing. The dark, bony hand continued to beckon from the folds of his flowing robes and Jonathon moved forward. Almost before he was aware of the fear his father's words about not fearing the unknown again echoed in his ears.

When he was still at a safe distance from the bench a deep resonant voice emanated from the seated figure.

"Come to me and I will quench your thirst."

Jonathon was now really scared and wondered if perhaps this person was some kind of nut.

He replied,

"I'm not thirsty."

The figure said,

"You thirst for knowledge. Come. Hear me and I will answer your questions."

Jonathon felt perplexed as to why this man had chosen to speak to him but his hesitation was countered by the magnetism of the strong, clear energy emanating from the robed figure.

Jonathon attempted to study the hooded face of the man without staring. He had an oriental face framed by long white hair and a long, wispy white moustache that twitched whenever he spoke. Beneath this curious exterior Jonathon sensed a kindly old man whose warmth seemed to melt the chilly surroundings.

Cautiously approaching, Jonathon introduced himself.

"Hello, I'm Jonathon."

The old man's clear, strong voice was visible as small clouds of mist in the icy air.

"I have been waiting for you. It is almost the winter solstice. I am here to teach you."

Puzzled that this old man appeared to know him and had expected his arrival, Jonathon said,

"I'm new to this town and just checking out the park."

The man said,

> "You are here to learn of the park, the seasons and how they relate to every man, woman and child on this planet."

> "But I don't know anything about this place. I've just arrived," he argued.

The reply was immediate.

> "That is why I am here — to teach you. Do not be concerned, let us drink together from the fountain of knowledge."

Jonathon was confused and uncomfortable in these surroundings but at the same time he was mesmerised by the strength and vitality of this man who seemed to know so much. The only thing he was certain about was that in some way the energy of this stranger was compelling.

> "Okay, what do you want me to do?" he finally said.

> "Relax", the old man replied. "Meet me here tomorrow, on the winter solstice and we will begin our journey."

Jonathon stared at the old man before gathering up the strength to ask,

> "Um...can I bring my friend Taylor with me?"

The old man replied,

"How old is he?"

"Fifteen, I think."

The old man simply said,

"He may come."

Jonathon stood and looked intently at the face of the old man, wondering what to do next.

The old man seemed to read his mind.

"You are confused and do not know me. Walk with me and I will show you the answers to some of your questions."

Cautious, yet curious, Jonathon followed him into the rapidly encroaching dusk.

The sun had long since set when Jonathon found himself standing once again near the empty park bench. Immersed in his thoughts and desperate to understand what the old man had just shown him, he dropped exhausted onto the bench.

He barely noticed the person clad in an overcoat and hat walking towards him. He jumped as a voice penetrated his reverie and it slowly began to register that someone was seated beside him.

"Jono, are you okay? You're wringing wet."

Momentarily stunned, Jonathon turned to his right and exclaimed,

"Dad!"

"I knew I'd find you here. I was worried about you. What's happened?"

Jonathon looked at me in surprise. The omnipresent vision of the shrouded figure silhouetted against the mouth of the cave still dominated his vision. The old man had bowed in reverence to the figure and Jonathon hadn't even noticed that he was being drenched by spray from the waterfall. When the figure had turned those glowing eyes directly on him it felt like they penetrated his very soul.

Finally Jonathon found some words.

"Dad, I...I've been at the waterfall. That's why I'm wet."

"In the dark? Why?"

Staring blankly into the evening mist Jonathon mumbled,

"I...can't really tell you. I'm sworn to secrecy, except I think I might be allowed to talk to Taylor about it. But I promise you I'm okay...I swear I'm not in any trouble."

My expression glazed over as unbidden images flooded in from the distant past. A fleeting smile turned up the corners of my mouth as I stood up, put an arm across Jonathon's shoulders and said,

"Okay, let's go home."

Jonathon knew in that moment that he was safe and that he would meet the old man again.

Later that night I chose my moment carefully and casually enquired,

"What were you doing in the park Jono?"

Jonathon's hands fidgeted and with his gaze still averted, he said,

"Well, I met this old man and he is going to teach Taylor and me stuff."

He seemed to be waiting for me and he took me to a place in the park that even Taylor doesn't know about. I can't really talk about it, but he seems harmless, so I'm figuring we can't really get into any trouble."

Something over-rode my initial suspicion and a completely different question emerged from my mouth in slow and measured words.

"Is he...an old Chinese man?"

Jonathon's eyes flicked open.

"How would you know that?"

I said to him,

"Do you know what tomorrow is?"

"Thursday?"

"It's the winter solstice, 21 June."

Jonathon, puzzled, looked towards the ceiling and said,

"He told me to come back for my first lesson on the winter solstice. What does he mean?"

"The days of the solstice and equinox are days when there is a huge influx of energy into the planet."

"I know a bit about the winter solstice being the shortest day and longest night. But what's the significance of the equinox?" said Jonathon.

"As you know, the summer solstice occurs in the southern hemisphere on 21 December and the winter solstice on 21 June. The spring equinox on 21 September and the autumn equinox on 21 March. And of course, the seasons are reversed in the northern hemisphere," I continued.

"The equinox is one of two days in the year when the hours of daylight and darkness are equal. The spring equinox is the day when winter leaves the southern hemisphere and spring begins. Similarly, the autumn equinox is the change from summer to autumn and is another day of equal daylight and darkness.

The summer solstice is the day of longest daylight and the winter solstice is the shortest day. These days are not just significant as the changes of season but they are times when all of Nature, including the animals, birds and fish feel the energy of a new season.

People are also affected by this change of energy and, in ancient times there were important festivals that were celebrated around these dates. Some people still choose to celebrate the change of season because they understand that you can use these times and the days either side as a window or portal to set the energy for the coming season."

Jonathon went to bed that night with more questions than

answers and the next morning he stumbled over to Taylor's house.

Almost before they'd made it to the privacy of Taylor's bedroom, Jonathon blurted out,

> "There's something really strange happening in the park. An old man sitting on a park bench said he had been waiting for me, to teach me stuff. He says I should come back tomorrow. Will you come with me?"

As he waited for Taylor's response, Jonathon surveyed the room. To get to the bed, he'd had to step around a huge pile of discarded clothes and then over Taylor's bike. His shock at the state of Taylor's bedroom was pushed aside by the immediacy of his concerns about the old man.

Taylor was lost in his own thoughts, miffed that Jonathon had discovered something in the park that he didn't know about.

> "I don't really think so," was his cool response. "I have homework to do and to be honest, I'm a bit freaked out by the way you're carrying on. Take a look at yourself!"

> "Please Taylor, I don't want to go alone and I hate to admit it, but I'm a bit scared."

Taylor was more than a little concerned himself but figured that since he was older and Jonathon had confided in him he was in some way now responsible for Jonathon's safety.

> "Okay. But I'm only staying for a little while...and if I decide it's not safe, we're leaving."

Chapter 4 – The Element of Fire

Neither of the boys knew what was in store for them but as they walked to the park the next afternoon they shared a sense that something big was about to happen.

At the park bench there was no sign of the old man. The boys fidgeted, waiting expectantly. Suddenly he was beside them, yet neither had seen him approach. He sat on the bench, adjusted his flowing robes, and pulled back the hood that covered his face and long silver hair. His hands were tucked inside the sleeves of his cloak.

Feeling awkward, Jonathon looked at him, at Taylor, and in every direction before finally saying,

"This is my friend, Taylor."

The old man said,

"Sit," pointing at the ground.

Taylor looked down and said,

"But there's snow on the ground."

The old man said,

"Sit and learn."

The boys looked at each other then sat crossed-legged on the snow-covered ground. The cold wetness penetrated their clothes instantly and Jonathon felt it creeping up his back. However his excitement and anticipation easily outweighed the discomfort. Taylor was annoyed at being told to sit in the snow yet he too felt a strange pull to listen to the stranger.

The old man sat still on the park bench with eyes closed. He appeared to be relaxing and he breathed deeply. As they studied his face, framed by long, wispy silver hair, they observed that his skin was quite tanned from what appeared to be many years spent outdoors. Despite his relatively aged exterior, his movements were agile and his eyes, when open, were deep and clear. Jonathon could not guess how old he might be.

After some minutes a long sigh came from the old man mixed with a huge exhalation of air. The boys glanced at each other again.

"You may call me Old Chinese. I have come to this place and time to teach you some of the mysteries taught in ancient China. The information I share is not found in your books but is learning from many thousands of years ago.

This knowledge was taught to the Emperor's son in the forest of K'an by the Lake of Li, beginning in his tenth year and ending in his thirteenth year. Once learned, the boy returned to the capital of China where eventually he used his knowledge to rule China in the ways of fairness and peace. These understandings were given to the Emperor's son by my ancestors within the beauty of Nature.

I will teach you young ones this information over a period of one year spent in this park, in discipline and silence. You must not eat any of your junk food on the day before you arrive and you must not discuss what you have learned with any other person until the teaching is complete."

That said, the old man stood and walked off.

Taylor and Jonathon looked after him, confused. Should they follow him or was today's lesson finished? Taylor stood, wiped the moisture off the seat of his pants and strode after him. Jonathon followed in silence. They walked towards the waterfall by the duck pond. Although Taylor knew the park well, he could not fathom where they were heading.

Passing the duck pond, Old Chinese continued on a few metres then stopped before a forest of large bushes and trees. He uttered words in what sounded like Chinese. To the astonishment of the boys the lower branches of the bushes drew silently back to reveal a path leading into the dense forest.

The old man stepped between the bushes, turned and motioned for them to follow. Taylor had no idea that this area of the park existed but he passed between the trees with surprising confidence. Jonathon, somewhat bewildered, followed. Once within the forest both boys looked back in an attempt to discover how the bushes had parted but there were no ropes or pulleys holding the branches open. As they watched, silently, but surprisingly quickly, the branches closed. Now in the darkness of the forest they wondered if Old Chinese could control the movements of trees.

They were now completely separated from the afternoon glow of the sun and engulfed by the imposing forest. Old Chinese walked at a brisk pace, confidently picking his way amongst ghostly trees and bushes, indistinct in the gloom. He stepped surely along the dark pathway beneath a canopy of overhanging branches.

Very soon an imposing fence of tall bamboo blocked their path. He stopped and again spoke quietly in Chinese. As if by magic, a hidden gate silently drew open revealing a glimpse of a most exquisite garden within.

As they entered the boys were enveloped in the beauty and grace of this hidden sanctuary. A small creek murmured between bushes in beautifully manicured flower beds set amid small patches of snowy white grass. A miniature arched wooden bridge spanned the creek and a path of stepping-stones led to a small home nestled at the rear of the garden. Branches of huge fir trees overhung the bamboo fence creating a canopy over the small timber and brushwood home, almost hiding it from view and imbuing it with a mystical quality.

"Come," said Old Chinese.

The boys entered the garden and before they could look for its mechanism the gate silently closed behind them.

"Our lessons will begin here," he said. "This is another of my Students."

The boys were surprised to see sitting on a beautifully hand-carved Chinese garden bench, a slightly plump woman wearing a bright red and orange striped dress. She was of indeterminate age, looked slightly unkempt, yet seemed completely at home within this beautifully maintained garden. Her friendly face glanced up in acknowledgement but she remained silent.

Old Chinese motioned for them to sit on a similar garden bench facing the one occupied by the woman. He bowed to each of them then sat in a rather grand looking timber chair with a high back that fanned outwards, somewhat dwarfing him.

Old Chinese sat silently for a number of minutes, breathing fully and deeply. Finally with a large sigh he began to speak.

"Today you will learn of the 'Elements of Man'. This information was taught to the Emperor's son in ancient China. The 'Elements of Man' is one of the 33 vibrational energies that control all life on the Earth Plane. First you will learn of the Fire Element and its relationship to the season of winter.

On the spring equinox you will return here to learn of the Water Element and the season of spring. The summer equinox will bring teaching of the Air Element and the season of summer and on the autumn equinox you will learn the last of the 'Elements of Man', the Earth Element. At the end of each teaching you will have the opportunity to ask questions."

The boys looked at each other and at the Student. Taylor wondered what they had let themselves in for. Nevertheless they were both intrigued by the energy of this man and his magical garden and soon forgot the uncomfortable dampness on the seat of their trousers.

After another lengthy silence, Old Chinese looked up as if from a trance. His voice seemed to deepen and his Chinese accent sounded more pronounced. His words flowed slowly and meticulously.

"Blessings and Peace to you all, and may the Living Spirit that comes forth in all life forms, in the four Elements of Fire, Water, Air and Earth, come into your life, and accentuate your beauty.

You must know that when you are deciding to reincarnate within this world, within your physical world, you choose reincarnation into the body, you choose the parents, the time, the place and the situation. In doing this you create within your life a new vibration within your world. You may reincarnate any time between conception and eight of your weeks after physical birth. The time that you reincarnate into the body signifies the Element that you will be in that lifetime. That signification also signifies the spiritual evolution or karmic effects that you will be dealing with in this life.

Man has four temperaments or four situations that he must work with, feel and be with within a reincarnation cycle. What each man or woman has to deal with will be one particular aspect more than the others. The first is loving, the second is emotion, the third is mentalness and the fourth is physicalness. Loving is the Fire of a sun, emotion is Water, mentality is the Air, and the physicalness is the Earth.

Depending upon the time you incarnated: Fire for the winter between 21 June and 21 September; Water between 21 September and 21 December; Air between 21 December and 21 March; and Earth, 21 March to 21 June. In the northern hemisphere it is six months later in each case."

Old Chinese paused, took a deep breath and continued.

"The four seasons. And man is like the four seasons. Man is beautiful as the four seasons, but at the same time must deal as Nature and animal and mineral with the four seasonal changes. And they become temperaments or reincarnational aspects.

In your world there are many varieties of Nature. No matter Eastern or Western, North or South, there is an Element of the four seasons in every situation. We deal with all of them in regards to each reincarnation cycle. Those of you that feel no closeness to the changing of the seasons, to the way

Nature goes, will find that by identification with the Element that is a part of your life, you will find an inner peace and beauty.

Each Element—Fire, Water, Air and Earth—has spiritual oneness within it. There are spiritual entities or a spiritualness separate from the Living Spirit, which is like your soul, but higher evolved. Man is likened to the Fire Element, animal to the Water, plant to the Air, and Earth or the material to the Earth. These four Elements are in charge of the four kingdoms in your world. Fire being in charge of man, Water in charge of animal, Air in charge of plant, and Earth in charge of mineral.

These are higher evolved spiritualities, unexplainable, and not having the words within your vocabulary to give you an idea of what they are, but they are beyond your reincarnation cycles and they are evolving within themselves for they too need evolution. And so by associating and understanding the time that you reincarnate, you will understand a little more about your spiritual evolution and what you will be dealing with within this lifetime.

The winter solstice is celebrated and has been celebrated in your Earth since time began, many times. For it is when the sun becomes again the stronger point, comes from the opposite end when darkness is more than sun and it is the birth of the sun.

All major religions have reworked and reinstituted their religion around the winter solstice between the time of the 21- 24 December in northern hemisphere.

This is a high time within vibration and within communication during your world. A communication that is beyond your understanding but not your feeling. To understand something is harder than to feel, and we are dealing with the bringing out of the feelingness of persons not the talkingness. Those born as Fire Elements have reincarnated to learn to love. Every situation that they face will be in regards to loving either others, living things and most importantly, themselves.

All in your world face the same aspect, but not in proportion to the Fire Element. The Element of the sun. A Fire Element must learn to love, and remember, love is not an emotion, and those in your world who try to make it an emotion are dealing within an incorrectness in the spiritual sense, for emotion is up and down and love must be consistent. But love is different."

Old Chinese looked at each of his Students in turn.

"If Old Chinese asks you what love was, we would have many different answers. You are incapable of loving the exterior, the soul or the subconscious of one another.

But you say, then what do we love? It is emotion that you feel for the subconscious or the soul, which are one and the same—it is not love. Love is a term that has been misused and we are using it in regards to the Living Spirit within you, the life force, the infinity, immortality, universality within you. That is the centre, that is what you love.

If you say "I love you" in your world, that takes on many different feelings. But you cannot say to the exterior or the subconscious or soul aspect of a person that you love them, for there is no way in a lifetime that you can get to know the subconscious or soul of another. But you can love and find a devotion for the spiritual self that lies beyond the subconscious or the soul, the Living Spirit within.

If you look at someone and you feel attracted to them because their eyes sparkle or the skin is soft or their body is what you may term in correct proportion, Old Chinese will note that when he was within your earth plane, body proportions were different than where you are now and those that you consider beautiful, in the time of Old Chinese would have been deformed.

But now we are dealing beyond that aspect— evolution, loving. Loving the Living Spirit within someone, not their exterior self—that is hard. You have no responsibility or no need within your world to respect the exterior or the soul of another, for that is their reincarnation aspect. What they are creating within this life, the subconscious or soul is what the five senses are picking up.

But you do have a responsibility for loving the Living Spirit within that person. You love the life force within, but not necessarily what is coming from their exterior selves. Your world centres on the interior that lies beyond what you are listening to now. That spark that you have felt from time to time, that livingness beyond your subconscious or soul. That is what you are to love.

Emotion goes out—when you look across a room and you are attracted to someone— that is emotion. Emotion goes out, love goes within. For if the Living Spirit is within each of you, to love is solidity by going within. For if you go within, you will touch the living part of you. Love cannot be centred or sent out of a person, it goes within.

So the Fire Element, that person that reincarnated at that time, needs to learn to love, not only all man, animal, plant and mineral, but themselves deep within. And also to learn that they do not need to feel that they have to love all mankind. They only have to love all Living Spirit. And so when you love someone else, you are loving the same thing that is within you.

If you are looking at someone also, that is different, that is their soul or subconscious and that is emotion that you are feeling. Love is different; it is feeling a spiritual affinity toward someone, not emotional, mental or physical, not the Water, the Air, or the Earth, but loving the life force that lies deep within.

It is easy to love a flower for it has beauty, or a tree for it has beauty. But what about poison ivy—can you love that? Or can you love the thorn bush that has scratched you? It has the Living Spirit within. The poison is exterior, the thorn is exterior. It is easy to love those things that seem beautiful and majestic. That is not love; that is respect. As long as it does not say anything and not hurt your physicalness, it is easy.

Old Chinese wants you to each understand that lovingness is within you, not without. If you are learning to love your fellow man and yourself, then every situation you get yourself in—you must love it.

You are Fire Element. But also the Fire Element is beyond that. What is the opposite end? What is the service aspect of a Fire Element? Fire is warmth. It is giving warmth to all living things and without Fire, all living things die without the sun. Without the warmth, the seed beneath the ground does not come up for the spring. You can go many days without water, without earth, in the soil aspect, or air, but you cannot go without the sun, without some of the rays hitting your earth.

The sun Element of reincarnation is to bring together the Water, the Air, and the Earth and to love all mankind and to serve. The Fire Element in its service gives consistently, for it is one that brings forth the bud, or the blossom, the harvest or the new things from the ground.

The Fire Element learns to love within and pull out the beauty through the exterior surface and allows the subconscious or the soul to feel the light within.

Those who serve who are Fire, serve in dedication. They serve in love, not having any material things. They are the key to most service in your world. For without them nothing else can live.

It is a high responsibility to be reincarnated Fire, for you learn to love and when you have learned, then you love and help others learn to love the livingness within themselves. Not by going out and changing their lives, not by being a missionary—there is nothing worse in your world than a missionary convinced that they are right."

He unexpectedly smiled.

"Old Chinese will take that back—there is only one other thing that is worse and that is a water buffalo in a rice paddy that has been stung by a bee. For, they are infringing upon the right of the individual to evolve within themselves. They are infringing upon your right within and no one has that right.

By loving yourself or the Living Spirit within you, you draw people to you because they see the same thing within you that lies dormant within themselves and they want to bring it out.

But it lies beyond their exterior or subconscious, and they are drawn to you. But if you go out, they see your exterior, not the lovingness within you. Old Chinese has said many times to many lessons, you are not your brother's keeper, you are your own keeper first, and then you become your brother's keeper automatically. That is the key. That is the essence of each reincarnation cycle."

Again Old Chinese looked at each of them and said,

"Running through your minds is, "Am I Fire or Water or Air or Earth?" Over the next four times you can make up your mind what you are."

There he paused, adjusted his robe and continued.

"Each has a sign and a reincarnational spiritual karmic aspect, and needs to learn something within each life. Neither one is higher or lower, for they evolve in a higher aspect, each in service. Each learning something, for if it is a Fire Element and they are learning to love and someone is an Earth Element, it could mean that they have learned to love, so do not judge in that sense. And of judgement, we will talk next time.

Fire...the sun. Within your world, within the physical aspect of it, if you want to in your farthest imagination centre on the Living Spirit, it would be the sun, but that is only a part of the Living Spirit—but it is a powerful, energetic cosmic aspect of the Living Spirit.

Fire...energy, power, a life, creativity, all things that gravity can circle around it; your physical world. Fire...learning to love and of all the Elements. Fire is the only builder. You have heard so many times, the only way that the world will learn next time is through destruction by fire.

Fire is love and it is through Fire that you learn to love yourself – you respect it, you feel it. The Fire Element always is drawn to the sun, is drawn to the ocean, to the waves because of the gravity and the motion of the waves.

The Fire Element always needs the sun and its expression. Any clouds or overcast will cause the Fire Element to feel trapped within. They need to bring the light without to themselves. The Fire Element is an extravert-ish Element, always challenging, but at the same time as soft as soggy rice within.

Fire revitalises, for if there is polluted earth, fire can burn it off and it can restart. Fire refurbishes. Fire can restrengthen Water to boiling, and it is only through Fire that the pollution aspects in your world can be overcome. And the pollution of Water, Air and Earth, if not overcome by the love of self and the Living Spirit within you, then the Elements will refurbish themselves by cataclysm and the changing of the earth's axis.

But man has the first chance by loving himself; the Living Spirit that lies within, the beauty beyond your subconscious or soul, the kindness within all life, with infinity, universality, eternity and immortality."

There was a long pause.

"You may ask your questions."

Astounded and somewhat confused, the boys looked to each other for support and then to their fellow Student. The Student sat impassively, apparently quite content with what she had heard. Jonathon was terrified at the thought of asking a question. He looked to Taylor, silently wondering if he understood enough of what they had heard to ask a question without making a fool of himself. Taylor's expression did nothing to quell his doubts.

A number of minutes passed and suddenly, yet serenely the woman broke the silence saying,

> "The Elements Fire, Earth, Air or Water—are they based on when you reincarnate? When you reincarnate, not the day you are born?"

> *"Peace."*

She then said,

> "You have spoken of the Fire Element as the winter solstice, is there any change in this aspect if one is in the northern hemisphere?"

> *"It is just reversed, the solstice is the other time, 21 December. Peace.*

> *But you must understand this. It does not change the cycle in aspect. It still has the same aspect—Fire, Water, Air and Earth. You must understand that in the western part or the southern of your hemisphere aspects, at one time, that was northern and had the same effect. The great pyramid in Egypt is always centre, 30-30 always, 30 longitude and 30 latitude. A perfect point—the 33.*

> *But you must understand also, that it is in the vibration of the Element, for in the southern part of your world, the winter*

41

solstice is the spring as it should be in the northern. It is just that those in the southern have shown in some way that they should not be different from those in the northern. For wherever you reincarnate you should take on the aspects of that nation, of that part of your world, not another part. That is most important.

But you have to understand also a spirit choosing a reincarnational time, chooses it usually separate from the conscious of the male and female responsible for the body or the form. For it does not want them to contribute to the vibration. However, at reincarnation there can be visions or bringing, or you will feel for the first time (the female) real life within your body, if it is at that time. The male will usually feel it within a dream state. In essence, the answer to your question is, Peace.

Love—not emotion, but love strengthened from within, that is the key to the Fire Element.

When the equinox is upon us we will be dealing with Water, the spring, but without Fire there would be no spring; without love there would be no bud, no life; without love of self, of mineral, plant and animal. Blessings and Peace."

The boys sat transfixed. Jonathon glanced at the Student and wondered what she was thinking.

After a long pause, Old Chinese spoke again.

> *"In Old China, there was a Sage sitting under the plum tree in the dead of winter, with snow all around him, piled up above his knees. The student was walking hurriedly down the road, bundled heavily.*
>
> *He saw the Sage sitting under the tree, "You're crazy! Why do you sit in snow under a tree that has no cover? Why do you not come into the village where it is warm?"*
>
> *The Sage said, "But I am warm. I have warmth. Feel my face." The student touched his face and it was warm.*
>
> *He said, "But come into the village. You will feel warmth and there will be people. Why stay out here within the forest? The animals are asleep, the trees are asleep."*
>
> *Then the Sage said, "The coldness here is on the outside. The coldness in the village is on the inside. I would prefer the warmth within and the coldness without.*
>
> *Blessings and Peace to you all."*

After a long silence, Old Chinese seemed to emerge from his trance-like state and looked directly at Jonathon for the first time since he had begun his teaching.

> "Go", he said, "Live your new understandings and come back on the day of the spring

43

equinox."

The boys rose without speaking and walked on trembling legs to the gate. It opened toward them as they approached and as they passed through neither boy looked back. Stumbling in the dark along the meandering track through the dense foliage of the forest, they were relieved when the branches of a seemingly impenetrable barrier of bushes silently opened toward them.

As they emerged into the dusk near the duck pond, Taylor looked at Jonathon saying,

> "What was that all about?"

Jonathon was too stunned to speak.

In hushed tones they began to dissect what they had learned. They recalled that Old Chinese had spoken about Fire Elements needing to learn to love, but they struggled to understand what that meant. Jonathon was keen to make some notes and explore this further but suddenly Taylor's attitude completely shifted.

> "Look Jono," said Taylor, "I don't know about you, but this all seems very unreal to me. Why don't we just forget about it all and not come back to the park for a while?"

Jonathon immediately cried out,

> "No, this is amazing information. We must record it. Why don't we try to find some of the people he calls Fire Elements in the park? Then we could talk to them and see if what Old Chinese says about them is true."

Taylor said,

> "No, I'm okay with showing you the rest of the park, but let's not get involved with this stuff anymore."

Jonathon was puzzled that Taylor didn't want to learn more from Old Chinese. However he could see Taylor's determination and Jonathon knew that no amount of arguing would change his mind.

Jonathon simply replied,

> "Okay, so let's keep exploring the park."

Chapter 5 – The Journey

Jonathon came home that night ashen-faced and confused and went straight to his bedroom. Seeing his state I gave him a few minutes and then knocked lightly on his open door. He was lying face down on the bed.

> "What's happened, Jono?"

He rolled over, put his hands behind his head and stared towards the ceiling.

> "Dad, I'm just not sure what I can say to you. The old man in the park has taught Taylor and I a huge amount of information but I'm not sure I can talk to you about it."

So, Old Chinese had begun the teaching and it was clear that Jono would not be able to discuss it with me or anyone else for that matter. He would just need all the support I could give him.

> "That's okay Jono, you don't need to share any details–just take it all in and allow it to become part of you."

He slowly turned his head.

> "Dad, how did you know what we were going to be taught?"

I thought carefully before I spoke.

> "Jono there are much greater understandings on the Earth Plane than what they teach you at school.

That's why I brought you here. We are both going through huge change and I felt there was a possibility that Old Chinese would teach you 'The Elements of Man'."

He gazed up at the ceiling, taking in every word.

"But this information is thousands of years old. It's unique. How did you know about it?"

I pulled up a chair, sat down and looked at him.

"Jono it was many, many years ago that I was introduced to 'The Elements of Man'. My teacher, T. Glynn Braddy, taught seminars about it and I have a collection of parables from ancient China on tapes at home. The information has always filled me with awe and understanding. I use the information almost every day of my life in my dealings with people. It has always proved correct and has never let me down."

He again looked at me and said,

"But Dad, there is so much to remember and there are no notes. I'm scared that I will forget half of it."

My response was immediate.

"Jono, you will not forget it. It will be with you forever. One reason why Old Chinese says not to discuss the information is so that the energy of the teaching will vibrate within your own energy pattern and will be absorbed, not lost."

"But how does this information relate to life? How do you use it? Taylor is losing interest and doesn't want to go back on the spring equinox."

I replied,

> "Every person who hears the information uses it differently. I cannot tell you how it will apply in your life because it will be different for you than for Taylor. He may choose not to go back. That is entirely his decision. All I can say is that it has been of incalculable benefit to me."

Just managing to hold back my tears, I looked my son in the eyes.

> "This will be your journey and these are your lessons–it's not for me to interfere." I paused, uncertain as to how much to say. "Did he have anyone with him?"

Jonathon seemed to ignore the question for some time, then turned and said,

> "Yes. There was a woman there who he called his Student."

I tried hard not to let Jonathon see my excitement.

> "Search her out. Look for her in the park and she may hold some clues for you–she has a special connection with Nature. If you follow your intuition, the park will unfold its secrets to you."

Jonathon, hands still behind his head, looked away and thought for some time. He then said,

> "Dad but how...?"

"Jono, life contains many unexpected situations. I often relate it to my sporting endeavours. You asked me once how I finished that Ironman with an injured shoulder. Well, life is a bit like an Ironman race. You'll learn from 'The Elements of Man' that not only are people representative of the four seasons but every event–even an Ironman–has cycles within it that correspond to the seasons of the year."

He looked enquiringly in my direction.

"I remember the afternoon before the race as I struggled into my wet suit, despite a maze of strapping on my upper body. I had waded into the cold murky waters of Wallis Lake full of hope. There in utter grief I found that I could not swim a stroke. I thought my dream was over and left in despair.

However, as usual, things had felt better in the morning. Before dawn, driven by something inside me, I was at the starting line. I prepped my bike, painfully donned my wetsuit and, when the gun sounded...I just swam.

Jono, your journey is to answer your own questions– it's not about my experiences. Be patient and you will learn what you need to know."

Later that night I looked in on Jonathon to see if he was asleep. As I entered his room Jono's gaze shifted to where I stood. I so wanted to explain to him that I too had once pondered the same questions that were now keeping him awake.

Eventually I left in silence as he stared at the ceiling.

Chapter 6 – The Salamander

It was July and Taylor continued to show Jonathon new areas of the park. Late one afternoon their wanderings took them to a remote area near its rear boundary. There they found the ashes of a small fire that seemed to have been carefully lit within a ring of stones. Intrigued, they decided to return after dinner to see if it was being used by anyone.

Several hours later they were once again heading towards the ring of stones. There, sitting cross-legged on the grass dressed in a long, flowing, and loudly-patterned robe, was their fellow Student.

She was gazing intently at a fire burning within the stone circle that emitted a powerful aroma that Jonathon couldn't identify.

Before the boys had made up their minds whether to approach the woman, she sensed their presence and silently motioned to them. Glancing nervously at each other they sat beside her on the grass in front of the small fire.

Her gaze remained fixed on the flames and without looking in their direction, she whispered in a warm and surprisingly friendly voice,

> "I have been waiting for you. Stare into the fire and breathe deeply of the incense. Concentrate on the flames."

As they breathed the sickly sweet air into their lungs each attempted to focus his eyes within the leaping flames.

"Look for a lizard-shaped object amongst the flames," she whispered.

Neither boy was game to speak or to run away.

Again without looking at them she commanded,

"Relax and surrender to your imagination."

Endless moments passed before Jonathon began to make out a lizard-shaped object writhing within the flames. He looked to Taylor who simply nodded.

As if she had heard their thoughts she continued,

"If you believe, you will see it. You are seeing the mythological Elemental entity known as the salamander. It brings warmth to the world. The salamander must be present before fire can exist. A match will not light a fire without the assistance of a salamander who appears immediately when evoked by friction.

There are many different types and forms of salamander besides the one you can see. They are rarely seen without a spark being present. Often they appear as small balls of light and sometimes as tongues of flame running over fields or peering into houses."

Her trance-like tone deepened.

"Medieval philosophers say that salamanders are usually lizard-like in shape, about one foot in length and often seen twisting and crawling in the midst of a fire. Others were described as huge flaming giants in flowing robes protected by sheets of fiery armour.

Another family of salamanders appear as indistinct lights floating over water at night. These were said to occasionally appear as forks of flame in the masts and rigging of ships.

Salamanders are spiritual entities who work with both animals and man by means of body heat from the liver and blood. Without this assistance there would be no warmth in our world. The salamander is the Elemental being associated with winter and is a representation of the person known since ancient times as the Fire Element. As you have heard from Old Chinese, the Fire Element is a person who is born for the purpose of learning to love themselves and others."

Taylor and Jonathon sat transfixed until the woman abruptly stood and departed without uttering a word of farewell. They watched her recede into the darkness, their jaws gaping, eyes watering and heads swimming from the incense. For long minutes they sat staring into the fire.

Taylor looked at Jonathon and said,

"What the...am I dreaming?"

Jonathon mumbled,

"I don't know. I've got to think about this."

Jonathon looked sheepishly at Taylor and said,

"All I know is that I saw that salamander. Do you think she was sent by Old Chinese to teach us more about the Fire Element?"

Chapter 7 – The Project

The boys found it difficult to integrate all that Old Chinese and his Student had taught them. Jonathon felt overwhelmed by the huge influx of energy into his life. He knew that the information they had been given was unique but he had no idea where it was all leading.

Jonathon decided that since he had been given this information he must be meant to do something with it. Feeling it was a duty to try and record it somehow he wondered how he might investigate further to see if it was true.

Suddenly his earlier thought returned.

> "Look, if Old Chinese lives in the park and teaches here, then there must be examples of people here who are Fire Elements. That is, we could look in the park to see if we can find some people who need to learn to love themselves, whatever that means. If we can find them, then perhaps we'll get to understand this stuff better."

Taylor reluctantly agreed although he still did not really want to help.

The next time that Jonathon raised the issue of documenting the information Taylor mentioned an assignment he had recently done at school that centred on comparing and contrasting two individuals who became famous for their actions during World War II.

He had not understood the nature of the project at first and had discussed it with his teacher after school. It seemed that she wanted the class to select two leaders or heroes from opposing sides of the conflict, and then explore the degree to which their background and personal qualities had influenced their actions.

Though he hadn't put a great deal of effort into the assignment he'd been intrigued by the differing qualities possessed by these individuals and some of his findings had stuck in his mind and left him with more questions than he'd started with. He wondered how, for instance, two individuals who were born in a similar time, or who came from a similar background, might act so completely differently.

Why was it that one person might end up angry and seeking revenge, while the other might choose to help others who were in a similar position? He didn't understand how the German people had trusted Hitler or how the German Führer had been able to live with what he was doing.

Jonathon seized upon the opportunity to convince Taylor that the Old Chinese understandings may provide the answer to his questions.

Though Old Chinese had not talked about the physical traits of the Fire Element Jonathon knew that he had mentioned three other Elements, each apparently relating to a different season of the year. With this in mind Jonathon began to record their observations and findings in a large school project book.

One day at school it became clear to Jonathon that Taylor was losing interest in the project. After a rather heated discussion Taylor still seemed indifferent and was clearly affronted that there were others who seemed to know more about his park than him.

In desperation Jonathon said,

> "This park holds some secrets that you haven't yet been shown."

> "What do you mean?"

Jonathon mumbled,

> "I can't tell you until we finish this quest. When we are done there'll be more information for us."

Taylor barked,

> "What do you mean? How do you know? Are you holding out on me? What else have you seen?"

Jonathon's ploy to maintain Taylor's interest was working.

> "Let's just say that Old Chinese has shown me some things that I can't tell you about just yet."

Taylor exploded,

> "You *are* holding out on me. This is my park and I want to know what you have seen here."

Somewhat embarrassed, Jonathon said,

> "He has shown me some things which are truly amazing. He will show us both more later but we have to be patient. Please don't ask me about this again. I can't tell you."

Far from satisfied, Taylor had no choice but to wait. However, he wasn't going to let Jonathon think he was the only one who knew secrets about the park.

Chapter 8 – Henry

Taylor arrived late at the park the next afternoon. Jonathon was waiting for him outside the park gates. As he approached Jonathon said,

"Where have you been?"

Before Taylor could respond he continued,

"Hey isn't that Don coming this way?"

Without warning Taylor immediately said,

"Quick, it's ten to five. Come and I'll introduce you to Henry."

"Who?" said Jonathon.

But it was too late. He was gone.

Jonathon chased him along the footpath until they reached the large glass and steel pyramid-shaped building that was the Invercargill Museum.

Following Taylor up the steps, they raced past an open-mouthed female attendant standing beside a large sign saying 'ENTRY BY DONATION ONLY'.

Taylor continued around the first corner at breakneck speed leading Jonathon via a display on the history of Invercargill. The next room featured an exhibit of old ships. As he raced by Jonathon glimpsed one corner dominated by the stern of a huge old sailing ship complete with mast and a full-sized spoked steering wheel. Jonathon wanted to stop and examine it but Taylor sensed him slowing.

"Come on. If we don't hurry we'll miss Henry!" he called over his shoulder, as they continued to barrel down a long wood panelled hallway and around a blind corner.

Taylor stopped dead in front of four glass displays. Each had a clear glass backing through which you could see beyond to a grassy enclosure that was actually a fenced-off section of the park.

"There's Henry," Taylor announced in triumph pointing into one of the glass displays.

"It's just a bunch of grass."

"No. See that thing that looks like a log? That's Henry."

"So?"

Ignoring his obvious disinterest Taylor launched into a lecture.

"Henry is a tuatara. He is a rare prehistoric lizard that now lives only in the very south of the South Island. Scientists come from all over the world to study him and his family. He is really old and if you stand quietly you might see some of his family."

Jonathon stared blankly at the log and then at Taylor. Then, as if on cue, the lizard still almost entirely hidden by the long grass, moved its front leg—just once.

Jonathon continued to stare at the unmoving object in disbelief for about ten minutes but it did nothing. Totally bored and somewhat annoyed, he backed away from the display mumbling,

"I have no idea what this has to do with our project."

"Don't you get it? Henry is our connection to the past and the Elementals!"

Upset partly by Jonathon's blank response and also his own frustration at his inability to get Jonathon to understand, Taylor's emotions got the better of him. He turned and stormed angrily away.

Jonathon came home disturbed that night. Over dinner he refused to talk about his day and just stared down at his food. I asked what was happening but he refused to talk.

After clearing the dinner table I entered his room and sat down. Jono pretended to bury himself in his homework, but he could tell from the look on my face that I wasn't leaving until we had talked.

Eventually he opened up.

"Dad, Taylor showed me this ancient lizard today. He's all excited about it as if it's important. But the stupid thing just stood there and never even moved."

Without wishing to appear too eager I said to him,

"Was it a tuatara?"

"Yes. Taylor seems to think that the whole of New Zealand history is based upon that thing living in the Invercargill Museum."

I lent back in my chair for a few moments and contemplated an answer.

> "Jono, I don't know much about the tuatara, but I know that they are unique to this area and the locals rely on them as a vital part of their history. Think about it. If we didn't know what has happened in the past, we would have no idea what our future might bring. Life has many cycles, including our seasons, and history can be useful in providing us with some clues about the future."

Jonathon looked at me enquiringly but said nothing more. I left him alone to finish his homework.

Chapter 9 – Don Adkins

Jonathon had not slept much the night before. He'd been possessed by a strange energy since Old Chinese had spoken to him. He also felt bad about what had happened the previous afternoon and spent hours trying to figure out what Taylor was on about with Henry.

He met Taylor by the duck pond, as always, armed with project book and pen. Since Jonathon had initiated the project he'd had to take responsibility for carrying the project book whenever they came to the park. Taylor's reluctance to be involved was even more obvious after their encounter of the previous day.

They did not really know where to begin looking for Fire Elements and, after walking all over the park, finally they decided that the warmth of the coffee shop would be a good place to sit and discuss their dilemma.

They sat in the coffee shop poring over Jonathon's notes at an otherwise empty round coffee table when an enthusiastic voice enquired,

"What are you two up to?"

Taylor looked up startled and quietly mumbled,

"Oh no!"

He then dropped his head and looked squarely at the table.

Before Jonathon could respond a tall, kindly looking man put his coffee cup and saucer down on their table. He poked with a serviette at some coffee he had spilled then continued,

"I've seen you two in the park recently. What are you

doing? What are these notes and drawings you always have with you?"

Jonathon looked at Taylor. His face still pointed towards the table, it was obvious that he was not going to speak to the stranger. Jonathon said,

> "Well, we're kind of doing this project and we come here to discuss it."

Without being asked the man pulled up a chair and sat down. Addressing Taylor, he said,

> "So, what is this project about?"

Taylor looked at Jonathon and wondered how on earth he would explain the project to a stranger. After a lengthy pause he cautiously began,

> "Well, you see, we are looking at different types of people in the park and, well, like...how they relate to nature."

Taylor felt that he'd provided a very poor explanation and expected a blank look from the stranger.

To his surprise the man seemed interested.

> "I'm Don Adkins and I own the newsagency. I think I know what you're talking about. I meet lots of different people each day and I often wonder about people who have similar qualities and others, who you might think would be similar, but are completely different. The park is a great place to research—it attracts all types of people."

The boys wondered whether his questions were similar to theirs. They knew that they could not tell anybody about what Old Chinese had said, however they felt comfortable enough to talk to him if it was disguised as a school project. So Taylor briefly showed him some of their notes.

Jonathon studied their new acquaintance. He saw a cool, relaxed man, tall in stature with a high forehead. He seemed outgoing and friendly, and seemed to know everyone in the coffee shop. Taylor seemed disinterested to the point of rudeness.

Mr Adkins told them that he liked to help his customers and that some even came into his shop just to have a chat. Later in the conversation he quietly confided that he used to be a scientist, specialising in quantum physics when he worked for a large company. It had been quite stressful and he now enjoyed an easier life.

During the conversation Jonathon felt embarrassed that Taylor appeared to be ignoring the newsagent. He had always seen Taylor as extremely self-confident and was puzzled by his apparent discomfort ever since Mr Adkins had sat down.

Mr Adkins seemed to innately understand the nature of the project and appeared keen to help. He said that he came to the coffee shop regularly and would love to check in and see how their project was progressing.

> "Some of my customers come here to the coffee shop and if you like I can introduce you to them. I often chat to them about life's 'big questions'."

The boys were still digesting what he was saying when he suddenly called out,

> "Hey, Tina! Come over here and meet these young men."

They looked up just in time to see a petite and very pretty

girl striding past their table. She turned and looked blankly at the odd trio seated before her.

"Hi, Don. What are you on about this time?"

Mr Adkins said,

"Meet Jonathon and Taylor. They're doing a school project about different types of people. Why don't you sit with us for a bit and listen to what they have to say."

Tina, who apparently had nothing better to do, slid her coffee cup onto the wooden table and sat in the remaining chair. Her fluffy little white dog sat obediently on the tiled floor beside her chair.

Taylor, being older and closer to her age, felt embarrassed. Jonathon waited for Taylor to say something but it seemed that he was still uncomfortable. Jonathon said,

"Taylor and I are investigating the different natures of people who come to the park. What do you do?"

"I own the beauty salon down the road. I just love the beauty industry because it gives me a chance to pamper and take care of my customers."

The boys knew nothing about the beauty industry and although they tried hard to hide it they couldn't help gawking at the vivacious, young woman who sat with them.

"You know Don, I don't really know what to do. I have to re-model my shop and everything's OK with the bank loan but I'll still need to put up my prices. I love my customers and part of me just doesn't want to do that. Do you think my customers will still come to me if I charge them more?"

Don, eyeing the boys, said,

"Let's talk more later."

Without warning she dropped her half empty coffee cup on its saucer and said to no-one in particular,

"OK, I'm out of here."

Addressing both boys she said,

"You can come with me if you want to keep talking but I have to exercise Mitzy".

She stood abruptly and headed for the door with Mitzy in tow. Taylor remained rooted to his chair, pen in hand, pretending to be about to raise an important issue with Mr Adkins. Jonathon stood and followed her.

Though Jonathon was as tall as Tina he almost had to run to keep up with her walking pace. Mitzy looked like a prancing wave of white curly fur as she too tried to keep up. He soon realised that it was impossible to chat moving at such speed so he gave up and headed back to the coffee shop.

When he returned to the coffee shop Mr Adkins had left. He sat facing Taylor and said,

"What was that?"
Taylor, with his eyes still facing the table, said nothing. Eventually he looked up at Jonathon and said,

"I don't want to talk about it. Ever."

Jonathon could see that Taylor was upset and knew enough about him to realise that he would not talk if he did not want to.

Later the boys discussed what they had seen and heard. Old Chinese had told them that Fire Elements came to Earth to learn to love and to serve others. They wondered if Tina's reluctance to put up her prices had something to do with feeling her clients might not love her any more if she did. Perhaps Tina was an example of the Fire Element talked about by Old Chinese.

While reviewing their notes and coffee shop experience Taylor remembered something his mother had once told him. Interestingly, when she was younger she had resembled Tina in appearance. She had said that people learn to love themselves by loving others. Jonathon pondered this thought for days.

Though they couldn't be sure Tina was a Fire Element until they'd heard what Old Chinese would say about each of the other Elements, Taylor and Jonathon each suspected that they had in fact met their first Fire Element.

Taylor often questioned Jonathon about what Old Chinese had shown him that afternoon in the park.

Jonathon simply repeated,

> "Look, I met him first and he has told me to keep it to myself. When this is finished I know he will show you."

Taylor was far from satisfied but had seen enough to know he must continue.

Chapter 10 – The Room of Mysteries

Taylor and Jonathon continued to visit the coffee shop and Jonathon enjoyed talking to Don Adkins. Taylor still seemed uncomfortable in his presence but refused to talk to Jonathon about it. Tina made some appearances but she rarely sat still long enough to talk to them. Don however, really opened up to the boys and was always keen to discuss their project and various people about town.

Jonathon suspected that Don's interest in their project came from his feeling that the boys were working in an area that was close to his heart.

One afternoon in the coffee shop Don said,

> "Look, why don't you come by my newsagency one afternoon. I think I may have something that may inspire you in your project."

The next afternoon they walked to his shop. They were both intrigued to know what they would be shown however Taylor became hesitant during the walk. He stopped outside the shop though he had been there many times before. He seemed reluctant to enter.

To Jonathon the shop was unfamiliar. When they eventually went in Don asked his assistant to cover for him and took them into the storeroom in the back of the shop. Nothing unusual here—just a room full of newspapers, magazines and dusty boxes.

He then ushered them to a small opening in the side of the storeroom. He stealthily drew aside a black velvet curtain to reveal a small dark room dimly lit by flickering candles.

Bizarre religious-looking ornaments hung from the ceiling and old-fashioned dark mirrors nestled within an ornate altar. Every space was either overflowing with old books embedded in ancient shelving or cluttered with grimy photographs.

Jonathon was startled to see stuffed owls staring blankly at him while a bat's red eyes glared at him, upside-down, from beneath tightly clenched wings. Jonathon shivered.

"This is my Room of Mysteries," said Don. "Here I keep old manuscripts, unusual books and anything that I think may hold teachings to help me understand ancient wisdoms. They help me to appreciate the present. Your project intrigues me and I want to help. There aren't any books here that relate to your work but you can come in here at any time to look around."

The room held an energy of excitement and mystery. Jonathon went straight to the old manuscripts and books. He hungrily skimmed any book or photograph of interest and paid little attention to the puzzles and unusual artefacts.

Taylor seemed to instantly lose his reluctance and appeared mesmerised by the mysterious old trinkets and, particularly, the puzzles. Both boys became absorbed in the strange contents of the room and Don was left alone by the door. Later, when Don had gone back to work, Taylor kept interrupting him to ask questions about the puzzles and various other things he found in the room. He now seemed much more relaxed to be around Don.

After about an hour rummaging through the fascinating, dusty treasures Jonathon was anxious to leave. He did not want to be distracted from his own goals.

When they finally went out into the night air Jonathon said to Taylor,

> "What's the fascination with the puzzles? They can't help us with our project."

Taylor quickly responded,

> "Oh, yes they can. Solving puzzles is like a game of chess. Sort out the solution and you get an understanding of the mind that created the question. I'm going to find out what it all means."

Jonathon was not convinced, but felt uplifted by Taylor's enthusiasm. He thought for a moment and said,

> "Taylor what was that about the other day outside the park?"

Taylor said,

> "What do you mean? I wanted to show you Henry and explain some of our history."

Without thinking Jonathon said,

> "No, you wanted to avoid Don Adkins. In the coffee shop you were very uncomfortable with him and at the park you avoided him."

Taylor thought for some time and eventually said,

> "Look Jono, the newsagency was robbed last year and I know that Don thinks it was kids from school. Sometimes he looks at me like he thinks it was me."

Jonathon looked at him dumfounded. He said,

"Well was it you?"

Taylor was silent for a long time. He then mumbled,

"Well, I was kinda involved and I know who was the ring-leader."

This time it was Jonathon's turn to be silent. Eventually he said,

"Are you going to tell him?"

Taylor said,

"No."

Taylor looked directly at Jonathon and said,

"It has always worried me even though I played a minor role. I just don't know what to do."

Taylor continued to visit Don's shrine following their afternoons spent in the park with Jonathon and he and Don spent many hours discussing ancient rituals and understandings.

Chapter 11 - The Element Of Water

On the afternoon of the southern hemisphere spring equinox, 21 September, the boys waited expectantly by the bushes near the duck pond. As they lingered, they chatted excitedly about what Old Chinese and the Student had told them regarding the Fire Elements. They also reflected on their own investigation of the people in the coffee shop and wondered what mysteries might be revealed to them that day.

Suddenly, and without a sound, the dense branches parted revealing the dimly lit path into the forest. Taylor, before entering, looked around but could see no one that might observe them slipping into the forest. He plunged ahead followed by Jonathon.

They trod the indistinct path as it meandered between the bases of huge trees. The track was littered with decaying leaves and pine needles and was strewn with pine cones.

Walking confidently was difficult but their anticipation carried them on. Through the gloom they were soon able to make out the bamboo fence and, magically, the gate opened as they approached.

They were greeted by chirping birds and the chortling of the small creek as it wandered between the flowerbeds and disappeared towards the house. Buds and flowers blossomed everywhere. Grass now illuminated the garden in an extraordinary shade of green. Everything sparkled in the afternoon glow of spring and sitting on her garden bench, the Student basked in the beauty of the garden.

Old Chinese stood to welcome them. He bowed slightly towards them, hands joined prayer-like in front of his body. He motioned for them to sit on the bench. He sat in his chair, breathed deeply, closed his eyes and seemed to slump into a trance.

> *"Blessings and Peace to you all. And may the Living Spirit that comes forward in the four Elements reach the vibration that you are and accentuate it. Peace.*
>
> *From 21 September to the summer solstice on 21 December is the spring or the time of the Water Element. It is the time of blossoming. It is the time of the new bud— as a butterfly coming forth from the cocoon. It is a most beautiful time of year, of life, and of a reincarnation in regards to the year, in regards to your age.*
>
> *We are connected here, too, with the lifetime that you are now living and with the ability to understand the Water Element, or emotion.*

Those reincarnating between 21 September and 21 December are Water Elements and will be dealing with the four emotions – dealing with every relationship they have, with every lifetime experience, with every effect pattern that comes into their life. These four emotions issue forth and cause them to re-orient and review their life. The Water Element is emotion."

He turned to the boys.

"As a male, the Water Element deals basically with life in a creative way—being very creative in music, in art, in the basic ways of expressing themselves outwardly, but coming from within. The Water Element male feels great emotion in Nature, cries freely, and like the female, will have a constant battle with their weight, usually associated with the retention of water within the system."

Old Chinese now turned imperceptibly towards the Student.

"The Water female is the best mother. For those children reincarnate through the Water female that want to have the balance, that want to have expression emotionally, and that want to have beauty within their lives. Even though all reincarnation associations are going to be emotion, they are the best mothers, the best wives in many ways.

But because they are emotion, whether male or female, they must deal with a great amount of karmic effect. Unlike the Fire Element that must learn to love all mankind and themselves, the emotional Element must learn that love is not an emotion and that to command and come in contact with their four emotions is their basic effect pattern. And when they command it, they will find that their life is as calm as a mountain lake in the early morning."

He paused and glanced at the three as if to gauge their readiness to understand.

"There are four basic emotions. From these come many others. But there are four basic ones. There is fear. The Water Element will be dealing with fear. They fear in two ways. Most Water Elements will bring from their last life to this one a fear in regards to the way they died in the last life—what you call phobias. Whether it is of height or of being closed in, whether it is fear of snake or animal, it is usually connected with their death pattern with their last life.

Very seldom beyond two lifetimes ago. This is a fear that they do not have to worry about, for you will not die twice of the same fear or the same way you died before.

Fear is the bringing forth of the lack of being in tune in the previous lifetime, for you never die in an accidental way unless you are out of tune. And so the fear of being closed in, heights, heat, cold or whatever you fear, is usually associated with that life. So you will have to come to terms with it, knowing that you will not die in this lifetime the same way.

The second kind of fear is the fear of expression of self. The fear of not being accepted by others for what you bring forth. Fear of basically each and every day. But the fear of expressing yourself is the most important. This fear is basically the inability for you to see the livingness within you. And it also shows to you that you feel that others are better than yourself. No one is higher than you or lower. You are the Living Spirit within you and to command that fear is to assert that you are the Living Spirit and what you are within will help give energy and peace to someone.

There are many people in your world who use fear in a power settlement and they see those that are afraid to express themselves and they enslave them within their stronger thought pattern. To break that enslavement takes much energy and much concern but it is possible. By realising the person who enslaves a fearful person is the same as they. They are afraid also that they will not be able to express themselves in this life."

Old Chinese's voice slowed.

"The second emotion is anger. Anger is a

77

most difficult one to deal with by most. For basically what it is, is when you get angered at what someone says about you or to you or with you. If someone says that you are ugly and you get angered, it is because you know they are right. You would not get angered if you knew you are beautiful.

If someone says you have cheated them and you get anger, it is because you have cheated them, for if you have not, what difference does it make? If someone says you do not love me, and you get angered at them, it is because you feel you do not love them. Anger is that way. Nation to nation, person to person, group to group. Basically when one person points out a weakness in another one and that person reacts.

Let us say, physically you are the ugliest person in the world. You would make a water buffalo look like a morning dove. Then someone says, "You are ugly." But inside you know that you are beautiful, that you have the Living Spirit within, you can say, "I am beautiful." And if that person sees your ugliness, they are seeing your exterior, and we all know that it is the interior that has beauty.

Old Chinese can see auras in your world. Old Chinese can feel the vibration as they come forward. Those who say they are handsome or beautiful are almost the worst mixture of colours in their auras as you could think, for within it is most difficult. And so anger stems from the truth.

Let us say you have not done something and someone says you have. The only reason you would get angered is because you probably thought that you would like to do it, and if you did not, then there is no reason to worry. And if someone accuses you of doing something that you did not, then there is a reason for them accusing you. There is a feeling they are bringing forth, a feeling that you are exuding from the inner parts of your vibration.

There is another type of anger. It is the anger that you have when a small boy or a small girl does something wrong or tells a lie. What are lies? There is not such a thing as a lie. If a small boy says, "I am the strongest person in the world. I'm the king of the mountain." He is! Who are you to say and to know what worlds he has created within his spiritual self? Who are you to step into the pattern of the small ones? And if a small one says to you, "Be quiet." And you become angered at them because of what they said to you, it is because you say it to them. But if it was an adult saying it to you, would you have gotten angered? But the spirit within that small one chose that right. Chose every inch of what they are getting. The reason you get angered is it is only in a small child that you can see the Living Spirit freely.

You are not angered because of the physical harm. It is deep within that you are thinking the Living Spirit is being harmed. The same essence that is within you, that you cannot bring forward as freely and as innocently as a small one. They choose their parentage as you have."

His voice now deepened and stressed each word.

"Anger, the truth. It is the truth that you cannot stand to defend. If it is truth, it is not worth defending. If it is not, it is not worth defending either. The truth will stand and untruth will not.

The third emotion is frustration. Within this come many—greed, envy, hatred, all of these, accumulated into frustration. Frustration is simply going up to a wall and only seeing that you walk through it, but cannot. Not seeing another way out—there is never only one way. It is those within your world that say there is only one way, one path, one religion, that cause frustration. For if you come up against a wall and you feel frustrated, look to your right, to your left, to the top, and if all else fails, dig under.

Frustration—the inability to see other avenues out of a situation that you find yourself in. Whether it is jealousy or greed, whether it is hatred, it is the inability to see your way out of them. That is why you're frustrated."

80

Old Chinese stopped talking and Taylor, Jonathon and the Student unconsciously held their breaths waiting for the final part of this lesson.

"And last, the one that all are involved in more than any—judgement. There are three kinds of judgement. The judgement of self—guilt. The judgement of your fellow man—that personage over there did wrong. Who are you to say he did wrong and on what grounds do you measure? And judgement in the legal aspect of your world.

Judgement of self. Guilt or judgement of the things that you think you did wrong. There are no mistakes in your world, you do not do anything wrong. If Old Chinese said, "That person made a mistake." It is negative. But if he said, "That person had an experience." That is positive. Every mistake or everything that you think is a mistake, that word should be dug and buried. There are many others. For just the muttering of them brings a connotation of disparity. Now, you judge yourself, "I did that wrong." If you did it, you did not do it wrong, for you learned. If you did something, you did it because you were pulled to it, because that was your intunement at the time. There is no guilt you should have, or judgement of self.

And of course the hardest is judgement of other things, of other people. "He is the worst liar I have ever seen." How do you know? On what grounds do you make it? In what reality are you judging this? If you call him a liar, that is your reality, not his. "This is the ugliest day or the most depressing day I have been in." That's your reality, that is not a judgement that you should make. For some it is heaven and a rainbow.

Judgements have a tendency to put an aura of dismal and an aura of blackness around you. But you say, "You cannot go through life without making a judgement." That is not true. You can go through life seeing that you are pulled to what you are, you do not judge it. If a person does something wrong you do not say it is wrong, for he is doing what he should be doing. That ties in very closely with your legal system.

If a person kills someone, it is not the killer's fault. It is the person who he kills' fault. You pull to you what you feel. If you are robbed, it is not the robber's fault, it is yours. For you have pulled to you what you have thought, or felt or protected yourself against. If you would work on your in-tuneness, and everyone else would work on their in-tuneness, there would be no robberies or murders. For everyone would be at the right place at the right time. You would not pull what you are thinking or feeling. If you are thinking a certain way. If you put 400 locks on your door, you will attract 400 robbers. If you open your door and then all is well, the robber will not come in and take what is there. And if he does, then it is his, not yours.

Your legal system punishes the wrong person. Think of the person in jail that is reacting on the thought pattern of another. It is actually the easy or the cheap way out. It is harder for a person to be perfectly in tune and pull only good things to them than building thousands of jails. Watch the person that locks himself into a world and it will be infringed upon. Watch the person that lives in a garden of freedom and it will not be.

The more material things you have, that you keep yourself and you are not willing to pass on, the more judgement you'll be involved in. You buy insurance to protect you from being ill. Who said you are going to be ill? Some large corporation says you are going to be ill so you must go along with what they are putting forward or else you will feel guilty being not. You buy insurance to protect your family in case one of you dies. That means you have no faith within and that you believe your family is like the grass—it cannot take care of its spiritual self.

Judgement is the hardest. It is one that you must work with and realise it is one that you deal with every day."

Old Chinese continued,

"The four emotions. Those of you that are emotional Elements will deal with them daily.

You'll deal with them with every person you meet, whether you are positive or whether you have decided to be physical or negative. This is the relationship. But to calm these waters that lie within you is your growth.

Fear causes muddy waters. Frustration causes choppy waters. Anger causes stormy waters. Judgement—the water leaves. Your whole role is to make the water placid and clear so that when you look in you see yourself which is the Living Spirit and as pure as the water is, as pure you will be.

These emotions are the karmic aspect of the Water Element. These are the evolutionary or the spiritual working patterns that they will be dealing with. They also will be dealing with water retention in the body, expressing their emotions through crying. They will need to be near the waves, the vibration thereof. Too far removal from the water, they will feel closed in. They will feel and they will need the wetness, but they will also need the sun. For the sun pulls the water to them and then releases it and returns.

The sun and the Water Elements are good mating partners. For the water goes to the sun and then returns, it cools the earth. It is the best compliment, whether it is male or female. There are other compliments. There are great difficulties also.

Two Water Elements and you have a house

full of water. Most difficult. It can be done, but extremely difficult for you never get out of one flood before you approach another.

And so what you are within you, whether you have fear, frustration, anger or judgement. Each Element will have a dealing with these, but the Water Element will deal with them beyond all other Elements. It will be their centre. It will be their main karmic aspect and many times causing many difficulties.

So emotion is not to be looked upon as something that should be steered away from, but something to learn, something to grow with, and to feel. Something to go beyond yourself. But most important, to centre on calming the inner waters that lie deep within so that you can see the Living Spirit in your reflection. In your reflection you are the Living Spirit within, you are beauty, you are life, you are eternity. Express yourself and you will feel freedom.

Blessings and Peace and you may ask your questions."

Once again the boys looked at each other in uncertainty and confusion. Questions formed in Taylor's mind but his mouth wouldn't form the words.

Again the Student was the first to break the silence.

She asked,

"In as much as an Element is determined by the time of incarnation or reincarnation, how does this affect the astrological premise today which is based on the time of birth?"

"All astrology dealing with the time your body comes into the world is physically oriented. Look at it. Look at when they work with you. Everything is related to your body, when you will do this, everything is physically or materially. We are dealing with reincarnation with the evolution of your soul. Astrology is not a solid fact that you need to rely and move within. You can regulate and move it any way you want. There is no astrology or particular birth pattern that you do not control.

And so those that say, "You are a Cancer, you cannot get along with a Capricorn." That is a negative thought. Who are they to judge that, who told them that's so? It is apparent that your world has allowed itself to give in, to judge itself by that which is unreal. There are certain astrological patterns that you should keep in mind. But you shouldn't let it regulate your life, for you are the Living Spirit and you control your universe. Peace."

She then said,

"Can you still have the Water influence and the Fire influence as well, or is it just one?"

"There are those who are born on 21

September and they are not Water. Most difficult. And sometimes they have both influences. They usually take on one or another more than the other. If it is born on the 21st, it is usually the sun or the Fire sign that wins out, but it will be one that will be a lot of Water, but the Fire will rule. Peace."

"Can you be physically born or come into your body, say in the Fire time but be Water?"

"You can reincarnate into your body any time between conception and eight weeks after birth. Peace. That is 11 month period. Peace."

"You said that Water signs, in general, needed to work out the emotion. Are there certain ways people who are Water can learn to help, to work them out? Are there general things, general ways?"

"Dealing with each of the four patterns, it is basically maintaining calmness and understanding why you get angered, why you judge, why you have fear, and why you have frustration. You must understand that you have fear because of a past lifetime death, or because you are not letting yourself come out of yourself, or that you judge because you do not understand that there are things that you will pull to you because of what you are, or frustration because you cannot get out of a situation or see other avenues, or anger because you react to the truth.

Once you see why these things affect you, then work on them. It is hard. But you must work on them with discipline in regards to affirmations. The best affirmation, of course, is:

I am the Living Spirit within. Each and every thing I do is for my highest good. I am complete within myself, I am perfect within myself. I am happy and satisfied within myself. I am one with all life within me. I am free.

By realising that you are the Living Spirit within, that you control your own emotions, and realising why you become emotional, then that is the way to work on them. There are those who will come into your world and will counsel you and will heal or say "I will show you how to cure your anger." And they will heal the effect, but they will not show you what caused it. You must see what caused it. A spirit guide will lead you in a darkened room to the light switch. You must turn it on.

For we could heal each anger aspect, each judgement, each fear, but if we did not go to the cause—what you must work on, then you would have no way of coming out of the emotions. It is by realising why you become it, and then working on it yourself with discipline, relaxation, and knowing you are the Living Spirit within. Peace."

Jonathon and Taylor were battling to keep focussed but the Student continued,

"Is anger never justified? What about cruelty to animals, or battery hens and calves? What could we do about it? Could we give money or can't we judge that–that it's wrong?"

"Why do you become angered at something that is in regards to its evolutionary pattern? Why would you become angered at an animal that is pulled to a man, or a particular chicken that is pulled to a man? You cannot make that judgement. You can basically see the reality of it and try to send peace.

But let me tell you one little thing about those chickens you have concern. There is a spiritual group within all chickens. It is a group spirit. The only way it separates and lets an individual come, is when man loves that individual chicken, bird or animal. Man walking by a chicken is enough love to cause a separation of the soul, and allow the chicken to develop and evolve out of his group aspect.

And so if there are three, four, five thousand chickens in a row, all man has to do is walk by and that is enough love for the chicken to evolve spiritually out of itself. If it does not, it goes back to the group. Peace."

She asked,

"Could somebody who is injured by terrorists innocently, by a bomb...are they attracting that bomb to themselves. What if a small child is crippled?"

"There is no 'innocently'. If the small person is within a certain area, they were drawn there by karmic effect. Everyone, no matter what the disaster, has the ability to step out of it, whether small child or not. From the time of birth to 12 years the child is reliant upon the parental pattern. They choose the parents and so what they are doing is in regards to that karmic effect. You cannot judge the body—it is the spirit.

Most children that die after eight weeks of birth and before 12 years, have returned to your earth plane for service and it is their last life on the earth plane. Most. There are, of course exceptions, but most. And they usually help the parental pattern. But if they are pulled with the parentage, that is their karmic aspect and you cannot judge it. Peace."

Jonathon felt that he must ask a question and so he blurted out,

"Do men need to eat meat?"

"Man has an herbivorous intestine, not a carnivorous intestine. Man's jaws chew up and down and to the side. All carnivores chew up and down. Meat putrefies within your intestines if there are intestines more

than two lengths of your body. Carnivores are one and a half to two lengths of the body—man ten lengths of the body. Eating meat is actually eating second hand vegetables.

But we are not saying you should or you should not. There is nothing within meat that you cannot get in the service foods—those foods that you can eat without killing an animal or a plant. The meat-eating peoples of your world are in minority and when the world began in this cataclysm, man and animal lived together.   It causes more difficulty than you realise. But those that are involved in that—that is their evolution and we cannot judge them, can we? Peace."

Taylor feeling the need to play his part said,

"Can you explain a little bit about fish in the sea? The bigger ones will eat the small ones and is that evolution?"

"That is a group soul. Man is the only individual soul and this is an instinctual pattern—something that is passed on genetically. Man develops his soul in regards to all evolution, and the only way mineral, plant or animal can evolve out of its species or out of your earth plane is by the love of man. That is the only way. Peace."

Taylor was now feeling more confident and asked,

"May I ask, how does...let's take a fish. If a fish is evolving, how does it evolve up to the higher fish that then is able to communicate with?"

"You must know that if it is a lower fish as a group soul, after many years it will have some association, some way with man or the products of man. Eventually in the lower Elements of this world, they will evolve out through the fish that man loves or gives attention to. A group soul is hard to define, but is an evolutionary pattern that may take 40 billion of your years. But since there is no time or space, why worry. Peace."

Jonathon then said,

"Then when we have pets, such as goldfish or birds in cages, are we actually helping them by giving them love?"

"You give them love and you give them peace, for they are concerned as you would be concerned for a plant. And the spirit will separate. Let us say that you receive a small fish, the group soul is within it. The fact that you begin to give it attention, the group soul severs and leaves a small soul within. It will evolve out by your concern and love. However, if you return that fish or animal back to its original place, it will return to the group spirit upon death. Peace."

Jonathon continued,

"I had looked upon confining a fish or a bird as not

being kind to it. Now, would you tell me how I should look upon it for its evolution?"

"If you love it, if you give it concern and if you help it evolve, it will be drawn to you for that. However, if you are in the situation of understanding the evolution of all living things, you will not be content with birds in cages or fish. This is an evolutionary pattern. This is a pattern that evolves.

Those personages that are giving love to a fish or a bird within a cage or within a glass are not aware that they are evolving a soul, but they are. Those that are aware of it will be very careful, and they will not put or constrict the entity that much.

They love by the recognition of growth. They can send love into an individual bird or fish and because of their understanding, and because of their ability to feel the evolution of things, they will evolve that through in a matter of a short period of time. Even within its freedom. Peace."

The Student quickly questioned,

"Are we helping to evolve the Guides, or have they reached the ultimate?"

"There is never a beginning and never an end. Guides, spirits, masters, mystics and saints come to your world to show you there is no evil, that there is only beauty. We

evolve by the service we are doing. We have gone into other worlds and other dimensions beyond your earth cycle. We are evolving. But the only way we evolve is by making you higher than me. And so we are not concerned in regards to the level we are in. Only that you will understand that you are beauty and the Living Spirit is within you. Peace."

She said,

"What do you think about Jesus Christ?"

"Old Chinese would like to teach you of the Nazarene, but the time is not here. He was born like you from parents like you. But you did not know that Joseph was 85 and that Mary was 15 did you? And that Joseph had had another family and that is where Jesus or the Nazarene's brothers and sisters came from. But that is another story for another time. Peace."

Taylor now feeling more relaxed, said,

"In regard to having cats and dogs and horses and other domestic animals, having them and loving them helps them to evolve, but what about if you have a horse and it runs free, versus say, the people that have horses and sort of ride them and train them. And sort of with a dog that you let it run free or if you train it to sort of 'sit' and 'roll over' and all the things and sort of different ways of having those pets?"

"If you love it, no matter what you train it or how you train it, it will evolve if you love it. Because does that training restrict them in the way that say a cage would restrict a bird? You cannot make that judgement, for animals are drawn to individuals for what they need. But at the same time as the separation comes forth, any amount of love or caring, whether there is constriction or not and if you understand it, you can do it the same as would the fish or the bird—in freedom. Peace."

Taylor continued,

"Now my cats...and if we love them, will they evolve to human beings or not?"

"Negative, we hope not. There are other evolutions that are better than that, other particular dimensions they can go to. Peace."

The Student almost called out,

"Is it not necessary sometimes, with regards to children, to enforce a discipline which is not necessarily based on spiritual laws but on arbitrary or social conventions which are not necessary?"

"If you are invoking that on them, they reincarnated through you to get it and so they need it. And so if someone is doing that, that is what the child needed. If someone is not doing it, that is what the child needed. There is not such a thing as a spoiled child. It is an evolutionary

pattern they needed. You cannot judge in regards to what one person is doing in regards to what you would do. Peace."

The words seemed to jump out of Jonathon's mouth as the thoughts were forming,

"Is there a specific way that people evolve through the Elements? Is there an order of evolving through them? Do you mean that if you are Fire, or if you are Water, if you are Air or Earth . . . do you need to be one before you can work with the other?"

"You usually start with Earth, then with Air, then Water, then Fire. But then you can go back and work with any of them that will help you. There are masters that are Earth Elements—you had them to work with plants. There are masters who are Air Elements. But you rotate through them initially in regards to your service and your growing patterns. Each of you that would be in one of these Elements it would be in regards to a service life. You evolve through the four of them before you get into service. Then you go into the others as you serve. Peace."

Jonathon said,

"I'm sorry, I didn't quite understand that. Does that mean that we would have gone through all four, then would come back into one of the four again?"

"You can come back into one, two or three, or all four. But it will not necessarily be in

order. *You go through the order at first. Peace.*"

The Student said,

"Does that mean that, say you are a Fire person, can you learn lessons from the other three Elements?"

"By being a Fire person, you love all Elements. That is your main effect. You definitely can learn by loving the emotions, the Air and the Earth Elements. That is true. You can learn by being with each, and the Fire more so. Peace."

Taylor asked,

"What does the spirit world think about heart transplants?"

"Old Chinese will not talk for the spirit world, he will talk for what he is taught. And the teacher that comes through him and from his Higher Self. For those that have heart transplants, that is where they are. That is their evolutionary pattern. But as you become more aware, you know you do not need it. You know you do not evolve.

In actuality, hospitals or anything like that is the easy way out, for if you can work within yourself, you will never have disease within your body. And if it is ready for the spirit to go on, no amount of transplanting will help it, will keep it from going. But that is up to the individual.

The person who is having the heart transplant—that is their evolution, that is where they are. That does not mean that you need to be them. There are many steps in the evolutionary pattern. Those who are steeped in the confines of a very strict religion are evolving as those who are in freedom. Each has its step—without the one below, he goes not to the one above. Peace."

The Student asked,

"Can you talk a little bit about what happens in the dream state? I'm confused."

"You must know it is in three levels. First, what you dream of daily, or what you do throughout the day or this lifetime— relationships with people and situations. Secondly, the nightmares that you have are usually in relation to bad food combinations or too much eating. And third, is when your soul travels in the spirit world, communicates with your guide and your Higher Self, and others who are sleeping, or others who have passed on.

This one is always in colour, the others are not. This one you will have the feeling; that when you awake you will have the feeling that someone you know is sick or have the feeling toward someone else—and you probably travelled with them in the spirit world. Peace."

She continued,

"If you do have that kind of dream, where your soul is out in the spirit world, can you work to remember it?"

"You will remember it as you work to utilise your intuition. These types of dreams come first through intuitive process. When you face the situation or the person, you will have a feeling. Act on it, and it will have been what you felt in the scene within the soul state within your dream. Peace."

Taylor asked,

"Can you comment on the extending of life by mechanical means?"

"No one has the right to do that. But let us look at two things. First, if it is within the medical or scientific field there will be an extension of existing life, as the person needs it, or is struggling with its physical self. But in regards to testing of creating life, you can create new life in your world, maybe a new baby, but that does not mean you will get a reincarnation.

For that is why Atlantis fell—they created perfect life form and there weren't any spirits in the spirit world that wanted to enter a perfect body. They needed to evolve, they did not need to be in a superhuman. And so the only ones that entered those bodies were the earthbound spirits that had not entered the spirit world—and Atlantis fell.

Mechanical extension of life is an evolutionary pattern of those who have it extended, for those that understand the trueness of life and its evolution will not need it. You will not have to be involved with it, or will never be in a situation where it will be used upon you. It is a stepping pattern, a growth pattern in your evolution. Peace."

The boys and the Student were exhilarated but also exhausted with keeping up with Old Chinese—a long silence ensued. When it became clear that there were no further questions, Old Chinese began his closing parable.

"In Old China there was a Sage looking over a lake, and teaching a student. And he said, "Look at the waves on the lake. You cannot see anything within it." And the wind died down, and the student said, "Now you can see the trees, you can see the rocks and the birds as they fly over. The water is deep, but it reflects beauty."

Truth is like the Water Element. Some is on the surface, some is deep down into the earth. But no matter who the personage is, the Water is there some place. You just have to search for it.

Blessings and Peace to you. "

The boys rose in silence and walked to the bamboo gate. They left the garden without looking back and walked along the darkening pathway to the outside world. They each felt an unspoken sadness in leaving the mysterious garden to return to what most consider to be reality. Emerging into the late afternoon sunlight through open branches, it was like returning from a dream.

As they emerged into the dusk surrounding the duck pond Taylor remained by the bushes whilst Jonathon started to walk away. When he noticed Taylor missing he returned to find Taylor staring at the water.

Jonathon said,

"What?"

Eventually Taylor looked towards Jonathon and said,

"Did you hear what Old Chinese said about being robbed? He said that if you get robbed it's your fault not the robbers."

Jonathon said,

"Yes I heard that."

Again Taylor stood staring at the murky water. Abruptly he started to walk towards the park gates.

Chapter 12 – The Swim

Jono came home pale yet, this time, looking more confident.

As he came in the door I asked,

> "So, how did it go today?

He pulled out a chair from the dining room table and slumped into it, propping his chin on his hands, wonder in his eyes.

Eventually he said,

> "Dad, it's amazing. It all feels so real."

I looked at him and said,

> "Did you learn about spring and Water?"

> He nodded.

> "Did Taylor go with you?"

> Again he nodded.

Wanting to keep the conversation going I said without thinking,

> "Jono, Water Elements can be a bit confusing for us. They often have too much emotion for us to handle."

Jonathon thought for a moment and then shot back at me,

> "So what Element am I? Do you know what Element I

am? Are we the same Element?"

Realising that I may have made an inappropriate judgement and given away a bit too much, I backed off.

"It's not for me to tell you what Element you are. You'll work it out after you have heard about all four. In fact, after you come to understand the four Elements you'll discover that most people are a combination of two Elements. But that all comes later. For the moment you need to concentrate on the primary four."

Jono looked at me for a long time and then said,

"Dad, there was so much information. I am so scared I will forget it."

"No, you won't forget it Jonathon—it settles into your subconscious and we all remember it in our own way. If you choose to remember your connection to Nature and begin to observe how the Elements show up in so many aspects of daily life, then you can never forget it.

One way to see how 'The Elements of Man' translates into everyday life is to apply it to something you love. Remember how I started telling you about that Ironman race when I was injured? Well, I used to look at a race through the paradigm of the Elements and see the seasons in it. You know, I had that injury before the race and you saw the stress I went through beforehand. As I have said, the preparation for a race like that is very difficult and stressful.

The preparation is almost more important than the race itself. You must train for many months. But you

104

also need to use your intuition to envision what's going to happen during the race. You have to create your race at all levels–you need a strategy for how you best use your physical energy, how to get your sustenance, and ways of optimising your emotional, and mental or psychological energies.

You use your experience of previous races to guess what will happen during the race, but you never really know. You must prepare for every eventuality, from broken or lost equipment to running out of energy. Jono, it's just like the winter is for a Fire Element. It is a time where you need to draw on your intuition and your ability to hold a vision in the darkness of the unknown.

Then the start of the actual race is the swim—no prizes for guessing that's about the Water Element— and I don't just mean jumping into the water."

He looked at me blankly, so I continued.

"A lot of emotions come up before the swim—it's dark as the race starts at dawn and you know the water is going to be cold. It's a huge effort just to get into the water ready to start. And there are helicopters flying way too low—the noise and vibration is scary and made me really angry.

That year, floating in the water waiting for the gun to go off, I was scared my shoulder wouldn't work and that I'd be left behind. But a strange calmness came over me and somehow I just knew it would be okay.

It's often frustrating during the swim because you can't see where you are in the pack or even where you're going.

There's only the pounding of your breathing in your head and if you aren't in control, you can find yourself at the mercy of your emotions—and those of the other competitors. In that Ironman there were two girls screaming in fear of being squashed as competitors swam over each other near the buoys. I wanted to stop and help them, but I wasn't in a position to do that.

It's a long crazy swim but the biggest shock is when you stand up to run out of the water. After being horizontal for so long, it's a real challenge to stand, let alone run.

That particular year I entered the transition area only about two minutes behind what I'd expected before the injury. I donned my riding gear and was off on the bike before my supporters in the crowd even realised I was out of the water. I discovered later that they thought it was me still out there swimming—but it was actually a man with one-arm, who did eventually complete the race.

Anyway, that's enough of me for one evening—the ride is a whole other story—we were only talking Water here tonight."

Chapter 13 – The Undines

The boys were hoping they would once again meet the Student and that she might reveal to them information about another Elemental, like she did with the salamander. Their anticipation and frustration grew daily when they could not find her.

Finally one late September afternoon they came upon her, sitting amongst the bushes by the base of the waterfall. She sensed them approach and, again without looking, motioned for them to sit beside her. The waterfall seemed less intimidating than the fire and so they settled beside her on the cold rocks, shielded from the view of the people at the duck pond by some small bushes.

> "Stare into the mists of the waterfall and surrender to your imagination," she instructed them.

> "See the undines. These are the spring or Water Elementals. The undines live in the invisible spiritual essence called humid ether or liquid. Beauty is the essence of the Water spirits, and they abound in symmetry and grace. They control Water and this has always been a female duty. For this reason they most often appear in female form."

Taylor was hesitant but clearly saw the exquisite figures in the mist. Jonathon readily accepted the vision and thought that the undines were indescribably beautiful.

She continued,

> "There are many groups of undines. Some inhabit the mists at the bases of waterfalls, some dwell in fountains, and others live in swiftly moving rivers.

Some drip and ooze into marshes and fens, whilst many live in clear mountain lakes. According to philosophers, every fountain, every ocean and every body of water has always had its family of undines.

Most undines closely resemble humans. They are usually in female form but not always. There are many legends about these spirits and their adoption by families of fishermen. But in nearly all such cases the undines hear the call of the water and ultimately return to the realm of Neptune, the King of the Sea.

Undines are rather emotional spirits, friendly to us and fond of serving mankind. They are said to have saved drowning sailors and to have taken men to their homes on the floor of the sea.

Ancient poets have said that the songs of the mermaids were heard on the West Wind and that their lives were dedicated to the service of Mother Earth.

The undines are the Elemental representation of Water Elements, and Water Elements usually come to this life to learn to deal with emotion."

The boys could clearly see the undines outlined in the rainbow mists of the waterfall. These beautiful female forms seemed content and happy in their watery environment, and it occurred to Jonathon that the undines had mastered their emotions.

So mesmerised were the boys by the beauty and grace of the undines that they barely remembered how they got home.

Chapter 14 - Mothers

The following day the boys met and discussed their recollections of the previous evening. It seemed that they each remembered different parts of the experience, yet innately felt that they knew it all, even if they could not recount it to the other.

As weeks passed, new life was blossoming in every corner of the park. Deciduous trees were bursting into leaf, bushes were growing new foliage and grass was shooting up through the ground seeking light and warmth.

The biggest change however was in the water. The creek leading to the duck pond was now in constant motion as its waters began to cascade over rocks and around tree roots. Life had returned to the duck pond. Birds began to take an interest in the insects that were returning to seek the water. At dusk small animals crept to the water's edge to drink. It was as if the park was awakening from a slumber as the sunlight from the longer days thawed the ground.

Jonathon felt the need to identify a person that Old Chinese would describe as a Water Element. He wondered whether they would also find these people at the coffee shop.

One afternoon Don Adkins came in and joined them at their table after buying his coffee.

"So what's happening?" he asked.

Taylor said,

"Well, we think we have pretty much identified the

types of people who relate to winter. Now we have to try and identify the people of spring."

Don asked,

"What are their characteristics? What do spring people look like? How do they relate to the spring-time?"

Jonathon said,

"Well we don't know what they look like but they cry easily and are very emotional people."

Don thought for a moment before saying,

"Well, if you need to find the people who deal with emotion you should go to the play area out behind us where all the mothers take their children. They are always in an emotional state over their kids or something."

After what must have seemed like a fairly ungracious goodbye, the boys quickly departed for the playground. There, playing on the swings, slippery dips and climbing bars, were about twenty children of varying ages. At the nearby picnic tables sat their mothers, apparently relaxing and chatting to each other, but never taking their eyes off their children.

Wishing to remain somewhat unobtrusive, the boys sat on a cold sandstone fence that divided the play area from the coffee shop. From there they could watch the women and overhear their conversations. Though varied, the theme almost always related to their children and families.

After a few days observing the mothers, Jonathon felt he

was starting to understand what Old Chinese had been saying.

He said to Taylor,

> "Remember how Old Chinese said that the Water Elements make the best mothers? Check out these women. And remember how he said that Water Elements retain water? Do you hear the short woman saying that she only had to drink a glass of water and the scales shot up? And remember that woman saying how she couldn't lose weight no matter how much she exercised? Quite a few of them seem to carry a bit of excess weight, especially around their hips. Do you think that's what he meant?"

Over the next couple of days the boys overheard numerous conversations relating to seemingly trivial injustices done to the women or their children. The stories often generated emotional responses from the mothers, and the reactions seemed, to Jonathon at least, to just recycle the energy and stir up more upset.

There were also a few fathers who came to the play area with their kids. Some of them seemed to be quite sensitive and more connected to their children, while others just wanted to hang out in the park.

Sitting on the sandstone wall Jonathon was riddled with confusion. Although he and Taylor had observed men and women here in the playground who fitted the definition of 'emotional', they'd also met plenty of other emotional individuals along the way. Tina had seemed pretty emotional when she'd been worrying about her clients. Don demonstrated a variety of emotional responses when he interacted with his customers and he was especially passionate about his Room of Mysteries.

Jonathon began to wonder if they should be looking for any particular emotions or whether Water Elements were individuals whose emotions were out of control in some way?

As he sat pondering this question a slim young man of about twenty approached and perched himself on the wall next to Jonathon.

He looked across at their project book and said,

> "Hi guys. What are you up to?"

Jonathon gave his now well-practised reply.

> "We're doing a school project about people who come to the park. I'm Jonathon and this is my friend, Taylor. How about you? What brings you here?"

> "Hi, I'm James. I'm doing first year psychology at Uni. I'm here researching for an assignment on bonding between mothers and children under the age of six. "

Taylor's ears pricked up.

> "Most of these mothers around here seem to be pretty emotional around their kids—do you find...?"

James interrupted,

> "Oh, *all* mothers are emotional around their children. The trick is to watch what happens when you separate them from their kids. When you take children out of the equation, some are still incredibly emotional, constantly worrying or missing their kids and can't stand being separated from them. But

others are more than happy to have a break and have some time for themselves. It's amazing how the emotion drops away for these women when they feel like they get their own life back. It's like some women just love to be really needed and depended upon, and others get really depleted by it."

Jonathon wondered if the mothers who missed their children and fretted when they were apart were the Water Elements referred to by Old Chinese. For these women it was as if family was their career! Was that what he'd meant?

The boys left the park that afternoon feeling pretty confident that they were beginning to observe the different temperaments described by Old Chinese in the people they met in the park. Their project was going to plan.

Jonathon's mind kept harking back to what Old Chinese and the Student had said to them about Water Elements being emotional. He felt that they had found the Water Elements but he could not reconcile what Old Chinese had said about Water Elements needing to step above the emotion and to calm the waters.

Old Chinese had said that to step above emotion you needed to know what caused it. If this was the answer, it created even more questions, because he had also said that *all* Elements have to deal with emotion.

Even though Old Chinese had described the emotions, Jonathon was still confused. Finally, he decided that only when they learned how the Air and Earth Elements fitted into the picture, would they get clarity on whether certain emotions were specific to each of the Elements.

Chapter 15 - The Element of Air

On 21 December, the summer solstice, the boys waited expectantly by the forest near the waterfall. As usual they were nervous yet excited.

Without a sound, the Student was beside them. In the moment that they felt her presence, she turned and walked between the thick branches that had opened at the edge of the forest. They trod carefully down the shaded pathway toward their garden classroom. At the bamboo gate she paused as the gate silently opened and then walked inside.

They first looked to the garden. It was a different beauty to that of spring. Flowers in myriad colours shaded the hot ground whilst a mixture of fragrances excited their senses. The grass reflected a dazzling rainbow of greens and the small stream gurgled quietly beneath the bridge. Beautifully coloured butterflies flitted from twig to twig, whilst small birds darted amongst the bushes and flitted around the head and shoulders of the old man.

The boys soaked in the summer energy in the garden. Old Chinese bowed to the Student and then to each of the boys, indicating that they should be seated. He then slowly sank into his winged chair and breathed very deeply.

> *"Blessings and Peace to you, and may the Living Spirit that is in all life forms, in the wind that blows through the trees, in the air that you breathe, come forth and give you the peace that you need for your higher development. Peace.*
>
> *The Air Element that we are concerned with today is an Element that is most exacting and sometimes most confusing within your world, because of its delicate balance and how it's understood by most. You will find more personages in the male aspect in the Air Element within your world than any other Element.*
>
> *For this Element, those reincarnating between 21 December and 21 March, are here to learn to step above, to filtrate through the intellectualism in their life, to understand that they need not prove everything. Those that have need to find every intricate detail and see and prove it are indeed within one of the greatest karmic effect patterns that they have ever been in.*
>
> *This Element of Air is most confusing to*

those that are within it, for karmically they have to deal with these aspects. They have to deal with mentality, concern with their mental achievements, with the mental ability that they can bring forward. They are concerned with the mental attitudes and the intelligence quotients of their offspring and those around them. They are concerned with the colleges and the universities or the educational advantages that their friends have. They measure in regards to know-how and not in regards to experience or evolution.

They are concerned with the mentality of personages. Those that have mental disabilities they look down upon. Those that are involved in the spiritual Element they look askance at, from side to side, not trusting, for they are dealing in a world of mystery and what they would call fiction.

Mentality—it becomes not only an evolutionary cycle for them, it becomes a God. It becomes their fascination, their sensitivity, and Air becomes what your world is concerned with now. You judge in regards to the education of your small ones, to what large institution you came from, to what you know, to what you can prove, to what is true or not true.

Mentality is basically that the person in the mentalness is trying to prove truth to themselves. Truth. What is truth? There is no

119

truth."

As they had come to expect, he paused before emphasising the following words.

"You cannot show me one truth in the world that will stand in regards to someone else's awareness. There is no basic outward truth. For the more you get into it, the more untruth you will find. The only truth that you can begin to see or feel is inner truth and that your scientist or intellectual personage cannot prove.

Those who study the mind will come forward with patterns, with patterns of reaction and a fixation. They will say because you do that and this, because of your parentage you will react this way and that. This is fine for the evolutionary cycle of those needing it, but they are dealing with the subconscious mind and nothing beyond. And they are basically making up their judgements in regards to what many people have reacted on and not in regards to a spiritual intuition.

For if you react one way, if you walk down the street and every fourth step you hop in the air, a man who studies your mind will find an affliction or something that was wrong in your childhood, in regards to some others that they have seen. It is the same aspect as physical astrology. You are based in regards to what they have reviewed in thousands of others, not as an entity, not as an individual or a new reincarnating spirit.

Mentality. It is the hardest reincarnation experience to go through. Worse, and harder than learning to love, before emotions, for within mentality in those who are trying to prove their intellectualism they build stronger, higher walls than any other aspects.

You all know them, you have seen them. They have subjected you to thought patterns and feelings, and at the same time you find yourself within them from time to time. Judging whether that person has been to a higher education or their mental abilities or capacities, or isn't it sad that that small one cannot do this or that. Or isn't it sad mentally that they cannot co-ordinate their body. Mentality. One of the particular Gods of your world at this time that you must deal with— those within the Air Element.

But the mentality in proving truth, this is the key. Those that are involved in this must prove or must have proof. They seek it. They look for it. They must prove is this true or is that true? You react to your small ones and say, "Is that the truth?" And they will say, "Yes." But you know what they are thinking or what they have done and then you punish them. But it is the truth to them.

You cannot punish or judge anyone in regards to saying that it is the truth. For each person has his own reality pattern, whether they are small girl or boy or grown-up. And when they react or do something, whether they react in telling the wrong story—who is to say it is wrong? In regards to what Element? In regards to what legal system?

If a small one hits his brother and you say, "Did you hit your brother?" and they say, "No." You may say they are not telling the truth. In reality within that lie, they did not hit their brother, they reacted to them with regards to what they felt. They are in a different world. An adult cannot judge in regards to truth of small one and they must understand that the small world is much different to yours.

And if someone says something to you and you say, "I know that is not true, that person is telling me a lie." In whose context? In whose reality, yours or theirs? If they said, "It was a beautiful day today." And it snowed 42 of your inches, and you say, "That person is telling a lie." How do you know that person doesn't love snow, even though you may not? So perception in the mentalness in regards to what truth is, is usually what the person in the Air Element is dealing with.

The second aspect is intellectualising—which is beyond the mental capacity or mental. Intellectualising is usually, basically things that have been said, have been written down, that you can study and put in your mind, that are written in numbers or in words and you talk about. This person said this, this person said that.

Old Chinese has been within your world and has watched those within this garden's mental pattern. There is not one of you that can write in words what you think completely. There is not one of you within this earth that has that capacity. There are some that can do it closer than others, but you find in intellectualising that you want to follow or worship the word, or the written word; those that have set laws, that have intellectually said that this is the way, it can be proven, four and two, six and nine, square and triangle.

No matter what you might figure that you can put forward, we can disprove it. No matter what line you put, it is not a straight one. There are many things that you must realise. In intellectualising, do not worship the words or the readings or the writings of those that have gone before. Use them in regards to building blocks not quoting symbols, or not things to build your life by.

That is the same in regards to all of your Elements. There are those in your world who think by books. Have you heard them? I know this person who has said that, that person said this in that book, or this. Have you read this or that? This is what this person said. And there is not one of you here, that at one time had original thought and said, "I heard" or "I read" and then came out with the thought. Afraid that it would be judged so you put it on someone else. It is easier to rely on what has been written than on your own inner development. And the intellectualiser must deal with this."

Old Chinese waited a moment for the threesome to catch up with him.

"The Air Element. It is hard, most hard. And then finally within the three aspects of intellectualism is the intellectual spiritualist. If you see one of these coming, get in the fastest vehicle you can and go the other way. For they will cause you no end of turmoil within. For they can prove God.

Those who study what your world calls theology, the study of God. Actually, theology was created when man no longer had faith for they had to study what God was. They could not believe it themselves. And so, book upon book upon book, intellectualising what religion is, the reactions of it. What the Nazarene or Mohammed or Buddha or Lao Tse has done, would not only fill this garden, but hundreds of gardens.

The intellectual spiritualists, or those men who are studying God—that in itself is a frightening thought. Theology is studying God. In reality, that is studying yourself and those who study themselves, learn, but those who make a habit out of trying to format, translate, regulate, re-feel, re-do, have difficulty.

There are those in your world who say in regards to the Nazarene, that he said this and that and then they try to disprove this and that. They say he was this and he was that. There are those who say this version of the Bible is the best and that is the best. There are those who will use nothing but what your world calls the King James version, as the true version. Those basically that your world calls the followers of the true word will follow the King James.

Isn't it interesting that in the time of the Nazarene there was no 'die' and 'dying'? There is not a Greek word that can make that and that is what the Old Testament concerns. The same with Lao Tse, the same with the translations of the Koran and the Four Fold Path of the Zoroastrian record.

And so, those involved in Air have difficulty with thinking. They think too much. They intellectualise, they must have proof and if it does not work in proof, if they cannot see it in regards to the words or if they cannot study it in regards to God or its spiritual development, they are very upset. So much so that your world is gauged upon that now, upon the Air Element.

There are certain physical aspects of the Air Element. Most Air Elements smoke tobacco. Look at your world. It looks like one great Chinese bonfire. The Air Element has trouble with their lungs and breathing. Look at your world and its pollution. The pollution of air is at its greatest crisis it has ever been.

The Air Element has difficulty in regards to finding a mate from the other three Elements. And if it is a Water Element, you will have all kinds of trouble. And so you must understand the Air is basically oriented in regards to the wind or the breathing, to the feeling of breath. In your world now more personages are suffering from diseases of the lung and they are Air Elements, mainly. Also, in regards to breathing it is air that is polluted in your major cities, your towns and your homes.

Air, an Element that is most important, but how does one use it? We have told you what one must watch. How does an Air Element use it to effect? Have you ever heard a breath of fresh air? Like the wind that blows through the jujube tree and lets the leaves fall softly to the ground. That stirs in the summer and cools you. The Air Element that goes above intellectualism becomes the soft breeze, will move and flow and you will not know they are there.

The Air Element in its highest can deal with all Elements. It will be able to fit within them *all. For it moves the Water in softness, it moves the trees and the plants of Earth, within the sun of the Fire Element. It gives you a feeling of coolness.*

The Air Element that has stepped above intellectualism is the healer. The Air Element that is basically able to give a refreshing approach, be able to give you the calmness of a summer breeze. It is the Air Element that is the healer. It is the reaper of the harvest, for the Air Element in its highest force can step above intellectualism and become a free-flowing aspect, not having to think but basically working with all three Elements, knowing that he can work among them and with them and harvest their crops.

For the time of 21 December to 21 March is the harvest time. It is the harvesting and the air is tiring but when you have a cool breeze of air you are refreshed. And so the highest evolution of the Air Element is the harvester of the fruits and his ability to work with the Fire and the Earth in co-ordination. It is the pulling together, it is the refresher, when the Earth is still or the Fire is hot, it fans the Fire and allows it to burn higher. It gives a freshness to all. It is, as Old Chinese said—a healer. Air Element can heal and will be a healer. It will heal you in one Element only and that is going to the source of the cause and letting you dig it out for yourself. For you will feel so refreshed by the Element itself that you will feel peace within yourself.

Fire, Water and Air. These Elements are important. They give you perspective in regards to your spiritual evolution, not physical.

Because this is a physical plane, we emphasise those things that you will have difficulty working with, that give you a glimpse of what you can obtain.

How many times have you had someone walk by you or walk through a room that you felt freshened by their presence? That is an Air Element at its highest. But the sadness is that there are fewer Air Elements in their highest evolution than any other. For they have to step above the mentality. They have to step above it and it causes them more problems and concern. Not because they don't want to but because it is the Air Element that we find your world within.

And so the Element born and reincarnated is not only dealing in an international karmic aspect as an intellectual, but if it is born into a nation in the Western world, it is dealing with a nation that is intellectually inclined. And if it is reincarnated in the Air Element period, it is dealing with their intellectual aspects. Three ways—if they step above it, like all other Elements, they reincarnate from your earth cycle forever. Blessings and Peace to you all.

You may ask your questions."

As usual the Student was quick to ask her question,

"What about spirits who would revisit the earth."

"What kind of spirit?"

"A good one."

"They will not make what you might call social calls. Spirit that has reincarnated out of your earth cycle, which means no longer having to reincarnate in, will only return on the guidance or the request of higher sources of the Brotherhood beyond them, so that they can evolve within the areas that they are in and help the Earth cycle evolve itself.

In regards to those who are in reincarnation cycle, if they pass through the white light which is just outside of your basic knowledge—it is when you die—your soul has to go through the white gate—if they pass through that, very seldom will they come back. Those who experience and work with those who have passed on usually have a guide that stands at that white gate and sees the spirits in that way.

Those that are not going through that gate are earthbound spirits that you hear so much about, in your folklore and in your homes and in your large meetings. In essence that is true and it is false."

Jonathon felt moved to ask,

"May I ask, do whole nations go through Fire and Air and Earth cycles, or is it purely individuals?"

Whole nations go through these cycles. Whole areas go through these cycles. They go through the cycles but in a different way. Usually the other way around, not Fire, Water and Air, but basically physicalness, which is Earth, Air, Water and Fire. It has been written in more works than one that fire will consume your world. That means that evolutionary-wise when you get to the Fire Element, you will be able to evolve. Nations do go through them, but not very fast. Peace."

Jonathon continued,

"When you go through the cycles, do you go through sort of in order, Earth, Fire?"

"When you first reincarnated into Earth cycle, many times ago, you go Earth, Air, Water and Fire. Then after that you can return, not in order, in those areas that you need the most work."

"Oh, so you don't sort of go through each one and that's it? I mean you could come back as Water three or four times or something?"

"Most people do. Peace."

The Student asked,

"Old Chinese, under which sign was Jesus Christ born and what was his birth date?"

"The Nazarene, you must understand, was born a man, from parents like yours. There was no virgin birth or immaculate conception. There is only one book within your Bible that says this. The book of Mark is the closest and the most authoritative. It was written in approximately 45AD. Matthew was written in 126 AD. Mark does not mention the virgin birth or the resurrection.

The Nazarene, when he came into this world you must understand, reincarnated differently than most. So know this. The Nazarene was conceived within the summer solstice, reincarnated in the autumn equinox, and born in the spring equinox. Nothing like your world says. For before the Nazarene was the celebration of the winter solstice, the birth of the sun. This does not make it any less or worse. Your world has lost sight of a lot of these feelings.

The Nazarene returned as a Master. He was the reincarnation of Zoroaster, and that is why the connection with the Star. That is why the Kings came from the Zoroastrian part of your world. But in dealing with the Nazarene listen to the word, what it does, not what it does in regards to regulating your life, but to opening it. And you will see all of the Elements within this particular lifetime. Peace."

She continued,

"Old Chinese, may I say that I'm a little confused in that you've told us that our legal system prosecutes the wrong person. And you have told us that truth is relative, that there is no truth. How should one then be guided, by what ethics or what kind of conduct should we respond in a legal situation?"

"You must understand that you cannot basically step out immediately. It would be like stepping from hot water into cold. But let us review your legal system. If you have a robbery you have drawn the robber. Rather than prosecuting the robber, if you would work on learning and knowing your inner self, and having a positive aspect of all living things, knowing that it is not the physical, material world, you will not draw the robber.

And so, those that judge, those that prosecute, those that basically enforce the law are doing it the easy way in regards to your world. For it is harder to have inner peace than it is to hire someone to create physical peace. If you have inner peace, if you decide you no longer want to be robbed, get hurt, be involved in what you call accident—which there are none—then you have withdrawn within yourself and realised the Living Spirit within and you will find that you will not be dealing with the legal system.

This is hard for a lot of personages to realise, but you will find that you will never confront it. That you will in essence be able to watch it, to side-step it, to sit back and watch it go on within your world, but you will never be involved. You can work within it, you can watch its law, by basically being at peace with yourself you will automatically observe all laws, not worrying in regards to when you step where wrongly.

And so it is a change of thought form, spiritual for physical form. The confusing part comes usually when you realise that truth isn't judged in regards to reality pattern, but as you work on your inner self, you create an inner truth that is felt, and that is the Living Spirit. And as you move in those circles so you pull to you only those things that are right.

If you are driving and you have inner peace, you do not need insurance. You do not need to be basically observed in regard to the law, for you will automatically observe it within your inner peace, and you will move through it. If you need a place, you do not have to worry in a regard to regulation or what the proof is. If someone is going to have an accident, and you are coming upon the scene, and you are basically in a free flowing situation, you will not see the scene. It will either have gone on before you or after you.

You will not be called upon to judge. It is a whole area of development. Not removing yourself from the world, but stepping back and seeing it.

In essence, those who get in this area can throw around them an aura or a magnetic force field of protection and walk down the street and not be seen. Literally not be seen. You place yourself in another dimension in regards to other perceptions, that you perceive and see what is going on around you, and walk and give guidance in that regard. Peace."

The Student continued,

"Can you tell us something about Aquarius, the Golden Age which is coming and all the upset throughout the world?"

"Who says your world is going to get to Aquarius? That is not for 1100 years to 2100. Old Chinese will say this. If your world does not stop pollution of the Air Elements, of the Water Elements, and of the Earth Elements, you do not have to worry about the Age of Aquarius.

It will be a New Age, through a new cataclysm. It will not reach there for some reason, and Old Chinese is not pointing finger at you, for you understand this as well as me, so many people say, "This is the coming age. Cannot wait to get over the mountain." But the Age of Aquarius or the Aquarian Age is a physical astrological area, and physically you are not going to have to worry about it the way things are now.

But secondly, it is a New Age in one way. If your world learns not to pollute the air, the water and the earth, it will be in a New Age. But civilisations more advanced than yours have never made it. But do not worry. In the cataclysm Old Chinese will accept you with loving care and we will rejoice as we accept you.

Consider this. What greater reward could any spirit want than leaving the physical body in the great time of a cataclysm? That truly would be a magnificent experience, for you would see and feel things beyond your imagination. If it is an Age of Aquarius, it would be an age of emotion, after the age of Air, age of Water. Not like Pisces, but an age where personages could feel rather than think.

And most of your evolutionary cycle—Atlantis only got through the thinking stage, Lemuria only through the thinking stage. Many Elements within the Southern part of the Americas in the Teotihuacan area saw only too late, the thinking. Each time, spirits, guides, saints and masters came to try to point the way. We hope it would be a New Age, truly, if it came. Peace."

She asked,

"Could there be a cataclysm that would not involve all of the world, but only a portion of the world as we know it?"

"There will probably be. In any cataclysmic period, there is a shifting of the poles, and approximately 50,000 to 100,000 people survive. And so, not the whole world is eliminated. In a cataclysm, it is not basically in regards to the whole world. It is Nature renewing itself, before man completely eliminates it. Peace."

"Will there be another Master coming soon?"

"Your world says there will be another messiah. There has been one born yesterday or last week or 63 or 47, or there has been one born here or there. If you learn and you know the Living Spirit is within you, why do you need a messiah? A messiah works only for those who do not understand. If you understand, you will never know him. A Master is only for those who need them at the time. So do not worry in regards to what has been forecast or seen. If you believe and know the Living Spirit is within you, then you are your own Master or messiah. Peace."

"What about those who intellectualise and use books as a guideline?"

"If you are utilising books, let us say as a guideline, you will read here and there, and you assimilate the truth. Assimilate in

regards to not taking them completely, but putting together. Pulling together and getting thought forms. If you read something, review it in regards to your inner self. If it feels good, if you can feel it like an old piece of clothing, if it feels as good as taking something that you enjoy, then you know it is the correct thing.

But utilise it as a stepping-stone for your own awareness or your own reality pattern. For reading and pulling together of thought forms are basically to give you a perspective in regards to your own reality and to the livingness that lies within yourself. As you gain strength in regards to your own reality, then you will know.

There are those things that you have read that you no longer utilise. They were stepping-stones. There are things that you are reading now—you are listening to Old Chinese. Old Chinese is only a stepping-stone as many others are too.

Anyone, any thought or philosophy that says, "I am the end of the road" turn around and run the other way. For the stepping-stones are the ones you want, not the end of the road. For there has never been a beginning and there will never be an end. And you do not want to come to the end of the road in a time when there is no end, for would it not be most chaotic being caught in the end of a road within eternity, when you have so much *to experience and grow?*

Read completely. If it does not feel good throw it away. Even if the person has many degrees, or many spiritual thoughts, or has converted or helped a lot of people. If it does not taste, feel or seem good to you, go on. It must fit what you think. It must taste right. It must taste like the summer rice wine. If it does not taste like that then you know it is wrong. There is a feeling that comes within, an acceptance. Peace"

Taylor then asked,

"Which is the best religion on Earth?"

"The one that is within you. The Living Spirit is within you. That is the way that is the best. That is the only way. Peace."

The Student asked,

"Do you think orthodox religion as we know it, will become much simpler?"

"There are a great many doctrines. Do you not find that it is much simpler to accept the simpler things. Is it much simpler to live, just to eat and to have clothing and a shelter over your head, not worrying about having eggs or fish, or having grape juice from wine grapes that have been grown hundreds of years ago?

The simple things rule and maintain over long periods of time. Orthodoxy, whether it is Christianity, whether it is Judaism, Hinduism, Sikhism, Buddhism, they all find self trapped within one area. The more orthodox they become, the more freedom those under them seek. However, those that become extremely loose and liberal, the more orthodoxy those under them seek.

There is a median. And what is that? That is simplicity as you put it. Knowing that there is a discipline within. Discipline life in regards to its forces, that by respecting all living things especially yourself, realising the Living Spirit is within, and knowing that there is basically positiveness and beauty all around you—you are creating a simplicity. Peace."

The Student then said,

"Of the four Elements, as a Water Element I find it most difficult to communicate with an Air person, and I would like to know if there could be some guidance for a Water Element in relation to Air people?"

"Most intellectualising Air people cause the Water to become a storm. It moves fast and hard and so that is difficult. When you see that kind coming, it is best to relax and let your water go through in calm. Do not try to contain it. The intellectualising will be around you. They will come and they will go, but as you calm your waters of the four emotions,

they will not come across your water. They will blow breezes and if they have strong winds, they will not come near you.

It is your acceptance of yourself that you will be able to be with. However, if someone who is very intellectual causes you disturbance, causes your water to have a storm upon it and the waves to come to and fro, the best way to overcome the intellectual is not to defend yourself. It is not to try to basically say your way is the best, but listen, send peace and walk the other way. For every word you say back, the worse the storm becomes. For they will be trying to prove that your waters are not the correct ones. Listen to them, do not talk back. Then you will find them going to other waters that defend themselves. Peace."

The Student asked,

"Do we have a destiny pattern?"

"Your destiny pattern? Yes. You have the ability to step above your destiny pattern, above all karmic effect, above everything that you have in this world. To do that causes great amount of energy and strength and you have to realise, you have to burn all your bridges behind you. You have to say everything that is yours is everyone else's. You do not collect anything around you that you are not willing to leave, whether is material gain or friends, and you serve

whenever someone asks. If they ask of you give. Never judge and you will step above karmic effect and your destiny pattern. Peace."

"What about earthbound spirits and exorcising them?"

"First realise that the Living Spirit does not recognise them, for they are creations of your world, of the physical world.

Secondly, if they are earthbound spirits, to affirm your understanding that you are the Living Spirit within, that you are eternal, immortal and universal, that within yourself is the God Force, livingness, the strength, and you will protect yourself. For they will not bother those energies that will know and accentuate the God Force.

Negative transference or negative feelings from those people will not affect those that realise that it does not exist. For it only exists on the physical plane, and by realising what they are sending out, it is only affecting themselves and that you can step above. Then you have protected yourself completely.

However, if you find yourself in a situation that is most difficult, wear around your neck a symbol of divinity, no matter what it is. Protect yourself each time you sleep, or you relax or meditate with the light of a candle *and affirm consistently.*

I am the Living Spirit within. Each and everything that I do is for my highest good. I am protected, and I am always at the right place at the right time."

She asked,

"How can we help earthbound spirits?"

"First, you need to have a companion. They need to know that they are dead, for that is the basic thing that they do not know. You help them by finding someone like yourself who wants to work with them. And then through affirmation and talking with them in a spiritual sense, you send them on—seeing the White Light—and letting them see a beauty beyond. It is a very delicate thing, and if you do not have a companion that can give you the support, it is best that you do not do it at all.

But basically, if you find one around you, send love to it. Try words as you would talk, and say, "You are dead, you can go on." There is always one caution. No earthbound spirit will cause you harm. They can be lonely personages and if you become friendly with them, they will follow you wherever you go. From house to house, from place to place. Your best is to be firm and to say, "You are dead. Look to the White Light." If you want to work further, get someone to help you and do it as a team, and one can always be in control. Peace."

"Is someone who is in the resting clinic earthbound?"

"They are beyond the White Light. The resting clinics are for those who have passed through the gate, and cannot yet adjust, who do not believe. It is hard for them to adjust to the world here, for they have no conception that they have reached the gates and have gone through.

The White Light is like a great pillar of white light. That is why in your world here, some say it looks pearly, but it is a white light. And when they walk through it they are accepted by spiritual caring, and they take them and put them in an area of rest so they can adjust to this Element that is here. Peace."

The Student seemed to have endless questions.

"Are the spirits who help other spirits adjust, people that have evolved very highly?"

"They can still be in the reincarnation cycle of your earth, but there are always teachers who are out of it. It can be those who are preparing who have been friends and who have accepted it, and will help them over. Peace."

She continued,

"Why do some people cross themselves as in a religious ceremony?"

"It does the same as those who say, 'I am the Living Spirit within me'. It is confident, it is an assertion of divinity within yourself. It is utilised for those who are in that evolutionary pattern, and who need that at the time. It is the same as anyone else would affirm in regards to a sign or an Element. It has no great religious or no great spiritual meaning other than to affirm that the personage is aligned with the Livingness or the God Force that is within them. In that way it is an affirmation—and positive. Peace."

The questions seemed to have run their course and after a few moments of silence, Old Chinese began the closing Elemental parable.

"In Old China there was a sage sitting under a plum tree, and a student said, "From day to day we see the wind blow through the trees, we see the leaves move, the grass and the flowers, but we never see it. What, is it? You see the water, the fire, you see the earth, but never the air. Why not?"

And the Sage said, "You must understand, it is the Element that teaches you that if you have faith or belief within it, if you can feel it without seeing it, then you know that you can feel other things without seeing them. The tree feels it, and you feel it in your face and in your hair.

It is like life. You do not need to see, taste, touch it, to believe it. All you have to do is feel it. And that is what life is. Feeling beyond the senses you could identify with. Blessings and Peace to you all."

The boys rose unsteadily, as usual filled with wonder and confusion. They walked to the bamboo gate. The Student led the way along the path as it meandered between huge pine trees. At the final gate she stopped whilst the branches silently opened towards her. She waited as the boys left the forest then turned and walked back to Old Chinese.

As Taylor and Jonathon emerged from the shadowy forest they were momentarily blinded by the late afternoon sun glinting off the duck pond. Jonathon felt a gentle breeze on his check as it wafted across the tepid water.

Finally Taylor broke the silence.

"Cataclysm? The Nazarene? The Brotherhood? Truth? What is this?"

Jonathon replied,

"I'm not worried about any of that stuff. We know about three of the Elements now, so all we have to do is find out about the final one."

Taylor thought for a moment and said,

"He said it again. He talked about getting robbed."

After a delay he continued,

> "He says you can choose not to get robbed. If everything he says is true then maybe, somehow, Don had chosen to get robbed. Do you think that is why he has met us and is now helping us? Do you think he knows it was me?"

Jonathon could not think of anything to say. He simply shrugged.

Over the following days, despite their attempts, the boys found it impossible to articulate what they had learned. They could only trust that they were somehow integrating the information at a deeper level.

Chapter 16 – The Ride

It was dark by the time Jonathon came home.

He entered the room confidently, sat at the dining table and said to me,

> "Dad that was way cool. We learned about the Air Element and about intellectualising. That stuff all makes a lot of sense to me."

Jonathon sat deep in thought for quite some time and waited. Finally, he looked up and said,

> "Dad, do you think I might be an Air Element? We haven't learned about Earth yet, but the stuff he told us about Air seems to fit."

Wanting to keep him away from trying to examine his own Element, I quickly responded,

> "Jono, don't worry about your Elcment until you have heard the fourth. Do you remember what I said about that race?"

He said,

> "Let me guess...you're going to tell me that the ride part of the race somehow relates to Air?"

> "You got it! That bike ride was incredibly painful—I rode with my elbows balanced on the aero-bars of the bike. The roads around Forster are pretty rough and jarring. The strapping helped and the chill wind on my shoulder initially numbed the pain, but later it just throbbed.

Outwardly the ride is all about wind in your face and the tempo of your legs. But internally it's a myriad of thoughts going around in your head. Six or seven hours is a long ride and you must constantly think and monitor your effort to ensure you finish with enough energy to complete the run. You also need to carefully watch the road and think regularly about fluid and food intake. You must keep a balance."

Jono looked up at me and smiled, saying,

"So you don't fall off the bike?"

Though I got his little joke I maintained my outwardly serious expression.

"No....and yes. In life, not just triathlons, you need to maintain a balance between your emotional, intellectual, physical and intuitive responses to situations you come upon.

But just as importantly you need to keep an acid-alkaline balance in your body. I have talked to you about this before. If your blood stream is too acid you will be angry all the time. At the other end of the scale, if your blood is too alkaline you can go through large parts of your life asleep. Then you will not want to get out of bed and you will feel like you have not enough energy in your life."

"But how do you balance your blood?"

"Eating a healthy diet, with a mixture of protein, carbohydrates and fats is a good start. You need to understand the effects of say, fruit, as opposed to protein on your bloodstream. Training for an Ironman teaches you all about food and drink and

148

how they react in your body.

And if you maintain a balance emotionally and in
your thinking, that helps program your body
chemistry."

I sensed that I was losing him so I stopped. After a pause
Jonathon blurted out,

"Dad, you know, we're also learning about the
Elementals."

"With the Student?"

He nodded.

"After the winter solstice teaching she showed us a
salamander and explained to us how it fitted in with
the Fire Element. Then after the equinox she showed
us some undines at the waterfall in the park. They
were beautiful."

Concealing my delight and curiosity, I said,

"So, Jono, do we need to talk about the Elementals?"

"No Dad, she's a really good teacher."

The conversation was over.

Chapter 17 – The Sylphs

On a summer day in January the boys were wandering aimlessly through a hilly, grassed area of the park. Jonathon had a feeling they would find something but said nothing to Taylor. They had no idea what to look for, but assumed that there must be another being that related to the summer in the same way that the salamander and the undines related to their seasons.

Sure enough, on the top of a grassy hill there was the Student, lying on her back amongst the long grass, looking towards the sky.

She heard them approach and, without looking, whispered,

> "Lie down. Lie still and surrender to your imagination."

They lay on their backs beside her and looked at the clouds scampering past. Taylor was frustrated when he saw nothing. He said to her,

> "What are we looking for?"

> "Hush."

After many long minutes Jonathon thought that he must be dreaming. He was not sure whether the tiny shimmering bodies he saw were high amongst the clouds or were hovering on silent wings just above his face. She again whispered,

> "Can you see them?"

Jonathon admitted that he could. Taylor just lay on his back staring at them.

She told them what they saw were fairies or sylphs. She said,

> "They are the Air Elementals. The sylph has the highest evolution of the Elementals. It exhibits sight, hearing, smell and all of the other senses. They congregate in temples on mountain tops with the Gods, and have taken it upon themselves to guard humans from trouble caused by evil spirits.
>
> The ancients gave the sylphs the job of gathering the clouds and modelling the snowflakes. They do this by gaining the co-operation of the undines who supply the moisture. They are the most highly evolved of the Elementals, as the Element of Air is the highest in vibration. The sylphs live for hundreds of years and never seem to grow old."

The boys did not need her describe the form of the fairies as they had seen them at the movies.

She told them,

> "The sylphs often assume human form although almost always as a male. Their temperament is mindful, changeable and eccentric, similar to that of an eccentric man. They work within the gases of the human body and in the nervous system. They are often inconsistent and annoying to others. They have no fixed home but wander about from place to place as Elemental nomads, invisible to most, but always present."

The boys glanced at each other in complete amazement. They lay there watching the sylphs for a long time before quietly leaving in wonder.

Chapter 18 – The Birds

As the days became warmer the boys became more attuned to the Element of Air. On very hot days this was because of its seeming absence. They began to appreciate the cooling breezes that tempered the oppressive stillness of the midday sun. The afternoon breezes would ruffle the surface of the duck pond and birds delighted in swooping upon the air currents amongst the tall trees.

Sitting in silence on a bench by the duck pond, studying the ripples on the surface of the water, Taylor suddenly leaped to his feet, looking skywards. Jonathon, following his gaze, saw a large eagle gliding high on motionless wings.

"Come with me," Taylor said.

Jonathon followed Taylor as he ran towards the huge aviary in the centre of park. Mentally, Taylor had made the link between air and flying and wondered whether the aviary might be the place to find Air Elements. As they sat watching the birds they were amazed to see the new energy that summer had brought to the aviary.

The boys reviewed what Old Chinese had told them about Air Elements as they sat for a few afternoons observing the people who came to the aviary. Jonathon also reflected on the words of the parable about the Air Elements. He pondered about feeling things without actually seeing them.

From their vantage point, they were able to watch all the passers-by, and on one occasion they even spotted Tina flying past with Mitzy. But hardly anyone stopped here.

When no people were about, the boys continued their discussions, which were often punctuated by some uproar in the aviary. The parrots had made an art form of ruffling the feathers of their neighbours.

Jonathon was now becoming more confident that he could interpret the words of Old Chinese. He recalled from the teaching that the Air Elements were prone to 'intellectualising'. He discussed with Taylor what this meant. Taylor thought it meant thinking about things too much but Jonathon argued that you can equally get stuck in your head recycling thoughts when you are feeling angry or upset. And that doesn't make you an Air Element!

Jonathon wondered if it was his imagination or had Taylor blushed slightly when he'd suggested you can also think things to death when you have a crush on someone?

Jonathon also recalled that the Student had said that the sylph or Air Elemental was a loner and sometimes could be like an 'absent minded professor'. He suspected that such people live in their heads and their decisions are never ruled by their hearts.

Jonathon joked with Taylor about their school Principal and how they all fell asleep listening to him at assemblies. He was just so boring and seemed to talk on an altogether different level to the boys. That provided a big clue!

After much discussion they finally agreed that one tell-tale sign of Air might be when someone turns something simple into a complicated explanation defended with endless logic, rules and facts that bores you to death.

Taylor shared with Jonathon how he had once had to stand outside the Principal's office because another boy had called him a name and started a fight with him. Taylor had received no sympathy and they'd both been punished. He felt that their Principal never showed any sign of emotion.

As their afternoon vigils at the aviary wore on, one tall solitary figure stood out. He arrived alone and consistently sat on a bench at a concrete picnic table that had an inlayed checkerboard. He often looked up from his book to gaze at the birds and on occasions he removed his hat and let the breeze sweep across his bald head.

After watching this man for a few days Taylor was struck by how familiar he looked. His face and body shape were similar to Don's but there was something else he couldn't put his finger on. Finally he worked it out and couldn't wait to share his theory with Jonathon.

In his school project about individuals on opposing sides of World War II he'd chosen to research Adolf Hitler and Barnes Wallis, both of whom had been 'visionary' in their own way, but who had entirely different personalities. In his essay he had pondered why, for instance, Adolf Hitler had been able to have such a captivating effect on the German people at a time when, it seemed, anyone with any common sense would have realised the danger. It seemed to Taylor that Hitler, though misguided, was incredibly articulate and so was able to persuade people to carry out despicable acts.

On the other hand, Barnes Wallis, one of the greatest British scientists of World War II, invented his remarkable bouncing bomb at a time when Britain needed a symbol of resistance. He was able to motivate Bomber Command to develop and use an unusual weapon when resources and manpower were extremely scarce.

Taylor's mental image of Barnes Wallis was from the old

'Dam Busters' film. If this was a true representation of him, he had a personality very different to that of Hitler and appeared to be the classic 'absent-minded professor'. Though not a convincing speaker, through sheer persistence he ultimately persuaded the doubters of Bomber Command that an unconventional response to Hitler was, in fact, possible. Ultimately, his bouncing bombs were instrumental in ending the War by breaching the dams of the Ruhr Valley and flooding major German industrial works.

After Taylor had recounted all of this to Jonathon and described what he'd discovered about Hitler and Barnes Wallis, one question remained. Would their different temperaments fit within the Elemental types described by Old Chinese?

Taylor had barely stopped for breath, but now paused,

> "Jono, that guy by the aviary reminds me of Barnes Wallis in the film. I think they might be the same Element. And he has that same oval shaped face, bald head and long legs like Barnes Wallis and...now I think about it... like Don."

The man seemed to be a complete loner. The boys, though inquisitive, were uncertain about approaching him as he seemed so deep in thought most of the time.

One day, there was no other table free, so they approached the bench occupied by the man and Taylor said,

> "Um, do you mind if we sit here?"

The stranger immediately replied,

> "Oh, of course not, please sit down."

Jonathon carefully placed the project book on the table so the stranger could see the title, 'The Seasons Within'.

He immediately remarked,

> "That sounds like a sterling title for a project. What's it about?"

Taylor, faced with the usual dilemma, said,

> "We're talking to people in the park to see how they are affected by Nature."

The stranger said,

> "Hmmm...interesting. Let me introduce myself. I'm Edward Phillips. Are you planning to interview me? What do you need to know?"

In conversation they gleaned that he had been an aerodynamicist. Jonathon had to ask what that was.

Mr Phillips explained,

> "I used to design the wings of aircraft. I'm retired now but I still enjoy studying the aerodynamics of the birds. I think science still has a lot to learn from nature!"

A few days later, as they sat chatting with Mr Phillips, a tall, slender and fairly stern-looking woman walked up to the bench and said, "Mind if sit down!" in a tone that was more a statement than a question. She sat on the bench occupied by Mr Phillips but positioned herself so far away that she seemed to be in danger of falling off the edge. To Jonathon her personality appeared cold and unforgiving. She dropped her book on the table and pretended to read.

It was obvious however that she was not comfortable and, in an effort to make conversation, she looked at the project book and demanded of Jonathon,

> "What is all this about?"

Jonathon gave the usual reply to which she responded,

> "I am Miss Burstin. I am the head librarian at the library. I haven't seen you in there have I?"

Miss Burstin, they soon discovered, regularly came to the park alone to indulge her passion for reading, and, she said, just thinking. She always dressed in what Jonathon thought was an old-fashioned manner and wore her hair in a tight bun. On one occasion she revealed to Jonathon that she had never married. She seemed very knowledgeable but always seemed uncomfortable in the presence of the boys.

On afternoon she said out loud,

> "I like the solitude and quietness of the park."

Taylor slowly looked towards Jonathon and then said to her,

> "But the birds make such a racket, it's hardly quiet."

She glared at him over the top of her glasses and stated,

> "Usually the humans here are quiet."

The boys discussed what these solitary figures had in common and realised that they seemed to be thinkers who were strong on logic, detail and facts and who had a love of history. They also seemed to share with Don an oval shaped face and a tall thin body.

Based on the description of Air Elements given by Old Chinese, and their own observations, Jonathon wondered if Mr Phillips and Miss Burstin were Air Elements. Taylor was convinced that only an Air Element would notice the fact that he wasn't one to frequent the library!

Jonathon recalled what Old Chinese had said about Air Elements intellectualising everything. He also remembered that the Student had said that the sylphs were solitary figures. What was their lesson? How would they balance or get beyond their intellectualism?

Jonathon began to hypothesise that perhaps each Element's vulnerability was also a strength. Perhaps the intellectual Air Elements had to learn to also deal with emotion and learning to love. Did Fire need to master the intellect and deal with more emotion? Would self-love and the intellect balance the over-emotional Water Element?

Jonathon tried to discuss his theory with Taylor but Taylor's mind was elsewhere. In desperation Jonathon suggested to Taylor that he seemed more interested in secret meetings with Don and solving puzzles than he was in the project.

Taylor retorted,

> "Tell me what the old man showed you last winter and I'll take more interest."

Jonathon said nothing.

Summer afternoons often brought spectacular lightning displays heralding thunderstorms. Jonathon enjoyed the feeling of electricity in the air and observing the effect it had on the birds.

As the summer drew to a close, the boys reviewed their findings in light of the understandings of the three Elements that Old Chinese had given them thus far. Taylor participated but made sure Jonathon felt his resistance.

Jonathon felt a burning curiosity around what Old Chinese would reveal about the final Element—Earth.

But in his mind there was still an even bigger question remaining around the significance of the Elementals. He wished Taylor would apply his interest in solving puzzles to this one! Jonathon had experienced a feeling of being grounded but calm in the presence of these entities, and yet as creatures of myth and legend, most people would regard their presence as unreal. Why had they been revealed to him and to Taylor? He struggled to see their connection with the Elements as Old Chinese had described them. The only thing he knew was that Nature contained many more mysteries than he, or most human minds, could ever comprehend.

He longed to discuss all this with his father, but knew he could not—yet.

Chapter 19 – The Element of Earth

The boys waited by the bushes near the duck pond. Despite the gloomy weather of this March equinox, they were filled with anticipation. They knew that they were about to receive their final teaching from Old Chinese on the season of autumn and the Earth Element.

As if on cue the branches parted and they stepped through onto the now familiar path. As always, the gate in the bamboo fence opened on approach and they entered the garden, which was more beautiful than ever.

The leaves wore the colours of jewels graduating from light green, through yellow to red then ruby. Some leaves had already fallen and the breeze had blown many into the stream where they drifted aimlessly like an armada of derelict junks.

Old Chinese bowed silently to them and they assumed their seats. The Student sat on her bench attired in a bright green and blue dress. She acknowledged the boys with a glance.

Eventually Old Chinese began.

> *"Blessings and Peace to you all and may you understand the beauty of the earth for it is the earth that gives you substance for the life that you are leading. Peace.*
>
> *The Earth Element is a most important Element, equally important as the other three—for Earth deals with a situation of your plane that all must come to terms with. We have said many times before that the earth is the university of the physical experience.*
>
> *You have had reincarnations before this earth plane and now each of you have had at least eight upon this earth plane. You are learning to step above the physical, the material, you are learning that the aspect of the physical part of your world is what you are to learn within the reincarnation cycles. When you have learned this, you will step above the Earth plane and reincarnate out.*
>
> *Earth is the physical. Earth is the material. Those that are within the Earth, those who*

have reincarnated in this time are dealing on the physical basis. They have difficulty associating and working with sexual relations. Each and every part of their life is not only physically oriented, they have difficulty with their intellect, with their emotion and with loving beyond themselves.

We have said the essence is to love the Living Spirit within. The Earth Element in its most base, the ones that have to deal with the karmic relationship of the Earth Element. It is not that they love the Living Spirit within them, they love the subconscious mind, they love their bodies.

It is from those that reincarnate at this time almost inevitably, on their death, if there is or if there is going to be an earthbound spirit, it comes from this plane or this evolutionary cycle, for it is a physical cycle. Those that are Earth Elements will have trouble, as Old Chinese has said, dealing with sexuality. So much so that they will probably seek love through sexual relations, love through sexual identification even to the point of worshipping or caring for the body in such a way that itself becomes an outer God.

Two physical Elements or a physical Element that a personage who is dealing with, in an area or a relationship that is intimate, would have difficulty going above the physical. All sexual relationships will be that only, there will be no spiritual. It will be very difficult for *them to understand the mental aspect, most difficult. Those in this that are dealing with this constantly are basically understood and seen for they are in every society. They are the ones that are very physical in all action. The major part of their being or what they do is centred around material gain or physical gratification.*

And so you must understand, this is a most difficult plane to step above, for it is the one you first reincarnate into at the beginning of the Earth cycle and it is one that you must deal with time and time again. Each of you have had at least two lifetimes dealing with the physical in regards to your main, spiritual karmic evolution. It is one that is, as Old Chinese has said, difficult to align and understand for you do not want to intellectualise and you will have great difficulty working there.

The emotions will not be very alive because the physical person does not want to be emotional because it does not allow them to consistently be physical. And anyway, if you are concerned about making money or gold, you cannot let emotion get involved. How many times have you heard that?"

Old Chinese waited while the boys and the Student silently thought through their answers.

"The physical Element is a difficult one. Each of you have had a feeling of it. For like

Nature, which the Elements are a part of, one works very closely to the other. Each of you feels a little of one and the other, and so you can identify time and time again, whether it is the physical, whether it is the intellectual, or the mind things that you work with, or the emotions, or learning to love. Each of you have felt these in one way or another, but some have dealt with one or the other most of their lives.

It is difficult to understand that you are on the Earth Plane, which is an Element to reincarnate above the Earth Plane, and you must have this physical understanding before you come. And so you see the importance of it, of understanding and realising that a relationship cannot be just physical.

Old Chinese has said before that when two personages come together in a sexual relationship, it is for one of two things— either for procreation or for the spiritual evolution of spirits on the spirit plane. Nothing else. If it is for physical gratification, then you are misusing the sexual Element.

And so you take upon you a great responsibility and you'll realise and use sexual ability beyond the base physical plane, or Earth, that is, just to feel good. Most Earth Elements fight and deal with this in the worst way.

But then there is the Earth Element that has

stepped higher. That has gone above this and you know those. They are the ones that walk with the plants, that talk with them, that help them grow. They feel best in the forest and the mountains. They are usually a recluse, not liking to be in large groups but liking the companionship of the forest and the natural things of the earth.

When you see and talk to them they cannot verbalise what they are thinking, but you know that they are at one with self, for they can help a plant grow, or help an animal see. This is the height of the Earth Element, whether it is a farmer or someone who is in charge of the evolution of the forest.

An Earth Element at this highest moment is centred and geared towards eliminating pollution of his Earth Element, or the ground, not letting synthetics within it, as he has learned not to have synthetic thoughts confuse his physical growth.

They can see spirits—the gnomes, the undines, the sylphs, the salamanders. The undines are in the water, the spirits of the Water, the sylphs, the Air, the salamanders, the Fire, the gnomes of the Earth. They can talk and walk with these for they are one with the spiritual things of the earth.

That is surprising. There are fewer of those than there are the others who have had and gained the heights. For it is harder to gain spiritual enlightenment in the height of your evolution on the physical plane than it is realised. It is hard on the mental plane, or Air, it is hard dealing with the emotions, it is hard learning to love, but how many of you are at one with the natural things? That can feel the vibration, or the aura of a flower, understand the pollination of two plants? All this is the evolutionary step of the physical Element.

Of course you all say, "I know someone who loves and likes plants" — this is true but how far, how clearly will they be able to see the spiritual Element within. For every plant you love, the group spirit withdraws from it and the soul becomes individualised, and then you are responsible to continue loving that plant so it can evolve.

That responsibility is a high one for by man loving other Elements, other living things evolve. To help plants evolve whether it is a tree or a leaf, is a high calling but it is usually a lonely calling, for you spend much time away from those of your own kind. So you must learn that longings must be overcome through yourself. And that plants and flowers and the darkness and the fertileness of the earth is your key to your evolution."

Old Chinese stared into the distance, seemingly breathing in the four Elements before he continued.

"Each of these Elements, Fire—the salamander, there are spirits within it, those who evolve can see it, Water—the undine or perhaps you prefer mermaid, the Air—sylphs, and Earth—the gnome. These are Elements, these are spiritual entities and they can manifest into a physical form that you will see, that may look like a personage in the small, but does not have the same consciousness, for they appear so you can identify. And so they will appear in body form, not basically like a human, but so that you will see that there is an identical evolving soul within whatever they are from.

Fire Element is a renewal, for it does not pollute, it is in charge, it is evolution. Sometimes fire will break out in your world to renew and this is a spiritual evolution, not something that man has caused.

Whether it is with correction of earth through fire or through air in giving it breath and freedom to burn, whether it is with water to burn off the pollution that sometimes your world gives it. And so these four Elements— each of you started with the physical, then Air, then Water, then Fire or sun, and then you turn from one to another learning those lessons that you need to learn the most.

This is the physical world, the university of the physical. When you learn to free flow, you step above and you are no longer concerned about your material being, about *the beauty that others say they have in the physical form. For you see beauty in each and every person beyond themselves. Physical, earth, evolution, all a part of the temperaments of man. Of man's evolution in the spiritual form of what he must deal with within any one of his reincarnation cycles. Peace.*

You may ask your questions."

Jonathon, feeling relaxed and emboldened asked,

"Were the pyramids built by man or was there some spiritual force involved in them?"

"Both. The Great Pyramid was built over 80,000 years ago. There are those who said it was built within this cataclysm. They do not know rice from a water buffalo. It was built and has survived cataclysm after cataclysm. It is the evolution, the centre point of your world. No matter which way you tip your axis, the parallel that it is on always maintains solidity.

It was created by a combination of men realising high spiritual evolution at the end of one cycle many thousands of years ago. They put it together utilising thought form— able to reconstruct stone, move it by thought and place it by thought. It was there and they survived the cataclysm within it.

*Every time there is a cataclysm, always the
first and one of the most important
civilisations always begins near the area of
the Great Pyramid. It is a combination of
spiritual evolution and of man. Peace."*

The Student asked,

"Old Chinese, in terms of the Elements and the
response that each has to its environment, you
mentioned that Fire has a response to the sun and
the moon, of Water to water and of Earth to the Earth
Elements. I don't recall you speaking about the
response of the Air Element to our environment.
How is this expressed?"

*"Air expresses itself in regards to the wind,
to the breath of fresh air. It is basically in
regards to keeping air fresh. Whenever there
is pollution in the air, the spiritual Element
will move and not be there.*

*The Air Element is most necessary for it is
what you breathe. It needs breath and that
is why it is usually the one that smokes, the
one that has to deal with the pollution of the
air. It learns what freshness is. It learns that
mentality must be refreshed.*

*Wherever there is pollution of the air, there
will not be spirits of the Air, or the sylphs,
but you will find a great amount of Air
Elements in evolution for mentally they have
created the situation.*

The Air Element in its highest form, the Air Element that evolves, goes beyond and is able to use mentality in this way. They are able to utilise all thoughts in a philosophy, in a philosophic point of view. They are able to basically be the metaphysicians within your world. They are those who complete or put together the ancient wisdoms. They are in essence the call to mystical thought in the highest form for they have begun and gone beyond the mental state as they use it in combination with the spiritual.

The Fire Element uses love in regards to its communication, the Water uses emotion or feelings in communication. The Earth uses basically the plants and the animals. It is through metaphysics or the thought form of spiritual evolution that the Air Element adds the greatest force. Without Air you would not have the records for the others in evolution.

The Student asked,

"Has anyone asked how long the Earth will take before civilisation will come up again, because will we have to come back here?"

"Not necessarily. It is possible for you to reincarnate out at this time. Each of you that are here can do that. It is no small task, but you can. Those who learn and work at the end of a cataclysm, and the reason there is so much spiritual help, so much metaphysical understanding, so much mystical centring is

because these spirits are reincarnated at a time to serve and to evolve out. They have waited many times, many hundreds of years for this. It is a service time.

Those who come and teach and help those to care for a cataclysm or a changing time, if they survive and they are in the right place at the right time, then that is their last time on the earth plane. If they die within it and return within the first five hundred of the new years, that is their last time.

Each of you are at the end of your reincarnation cycle, even though you do not feel at times that you have, what you might say, the harvest in. There are a lot of precepts that you do not understand, most personages do not reincarnate out of the Earth cycle by being great saints or masters, for the saints and masters and mystics come back after they reincarnate out. If you learn your lesson here and it is the last one, you will go.

If the earth ever gets to the point where it must replenish itself by eliminating itself, then you will reincarnate to other worlds that are like the earth within your galactic system, that are going through the same evolution as you and you would not be too far off in understanding them. You will only wait for a period of time until the time was right. But that does not happen very often, once or twice, and it only happens in every

20 - 30 billion years of your earth time. Peace."

She continued,

"Is it possible to say, Old Chinese, on an average how many times a person is reincarnated in a human form on the Earth cycle?"

"Average nine, between nine and twelve. Most of you, depending upon the time you came into the Earth cycle. It averages nine, usually does not get more than 12, however, there are those that double 12 and this is a particular problem they are in, but that happens very seldom. Peace."

Taylor asked,

"Do you usually come as an animal before you come as a human?"

"You usually do not. It very seldom happens. It has happened and this is in regards to one of two things. Every once in a while there will be an evolution in the highest form and it will be a person who is centred on animals in regards to their particular growth pattern on the earth. But very seldom. That is entirely another evolutionary cycle and after you love an animal and release its soul, after it dies it goes into other planes.

Now, it is possible, this is hard for you perhaps to fathom, but let us look. Perhaps the plant that is in your pagoda is a potential human being seven or eight cataclysms away. It does not reincarnate out and back to man immediately, it goes to other dimensions, to other evolutions, other workings. For most of you have evolved and have been colour, even sound. So it is not in essence to the physical, which you are concerned with but it can be the smallest and even larger vibrations that you are aware of. Peace."

Jonathon then asked,

"Where do flying saucers come from?"

"Do not understand what you mean by flying saucers. Flying dishes? I do not understand."

"We call them unidentified flying objects."

"Peace. I understand what you are talking of now. These are not from worlds usually within your universe. They are entering in dimensional areas from other dimensions. They are vibrations that you can feel and see, but they are vibrations usually of light, but they are not necessarily physical. They can manifest in the physical but they are not from other planets, they are from other dimensions, other evolutions, other cycles, other areas. They are able to adapt and able to walk from one dimension to another, but they can never go from one dimension to another that will hurt that dimension.

So there will never be an unidentified object that is flying that will harm you. If you try to harm it, it will resist the harm, for it is understanding evolution and will not interfere. It comes in regards to seeing, to feeling. It comes in regards to perhaps giving enlightenment, that there are other dimensions, that you are not alone in a single universe. Peace."

The Student then asked,

"When you speak of other dimensions and other lives and things, is it possible to talk about that?"

"When you go and look up into the sky and see stars, there are one or two that you can see that are one hundred million light years away. That means one hundred million years it took for that light to get here—before the Great Pyramid, even before this earth was created. Now, it is possible that that light, where it came from is no longer, for it could be completely extinguished. But it would take a hundred million years before it would go out. That is the physical plane.

You are dealing with a galaxy with the universe of the physical. Physically you can look out and there is no end, it is not a circle, there is no end—that is the physical plane. The stars you see, the ability to travel within them is physical. The next closest would be atoms and molecules. For within an atom and a molecule there is infinity that way. So within a physical world you have an infinity. You cannot see atoms and molecules but you have the ability to break them.

Now, the stars you see are only a fraction in amount of the other dimensions that are even bigger than this dimension of the physical plane. Your mind cannot decrease. It is hard to have one. To realise by just one small step, adjusting the vibration, you are on another plane that can be larger in dimension and in depth than the physical, but there are hundreds and hundreds and hundreds of thousands of these dimensions in evolution. So how does Old Chinese explain them? Peace."

Jonathon continued,

"Is it necessary for man to go into space in order to discover all sorts of new miracles of Nature?"

"Man will go into your galaxies, will see many things, even meet other Elements that have gone before. There was a civilisation two cataclysms ago in approximately your Peruvian area that have gone farther than man is going now. That had satellites going around your earth that told basic time intricately. Their communication system would make your earth's communication system seem like sending messages by birds. Yes, it will go further but in the inevitability of cataclysmic change—not too far. Peace."

The Student then asked,

"Are there new discoveries being made about Atlantis? For instance, documents hidden in the pyramids?"

"Not basically about Atlantis as you know it for there are three of them, in three different times. But it will bring forth new enlightenment of a time before Atlantis. There will be discoveries in regards to this, but it will be after there have been earth changes and there is earth upheaval. Now, there will be documents discovered in the Great Pyramid in the future that will tell of the civilisations before the last cataclysm, but not necessarily Atlantis as you know it. Peace."

The Student continued,

"Where was Atlantis, in which part of...?"

"It was situated one time between your country of Spain and your islands in the Caribbean and what you call the hump of Brazil and the bend in the continent of Africa. Many times it split and had smaller areas but it had many different evolutions. Sometimes it was larger than your continent of Africa, sometimes smaller than the continent of Australia.

And so the theory that all of the particular earth parts fit together is true, for if you remove the water, it will fit together. It is just in the way it rises and lowers in earth changes."

The Student said,

"How, does the salt…"

"It absorbs, it absorbs what it is or what it is around. The sodium aspect is a make-up of not only the earth that has water along but also of the life that is within it, for the more plant life you have within it, the more sodium you will see. The more livingness that you have within it, the more salt there will be. There are areas in your world that are not connected to your ocean, that have more salt within them than your ocean water. But you cannot sink, impossible. This is in regards to the make-up or the mineral content of the earth in the area.

Now, you can go into the cold areas of your earth, to the hot areas of your earth and right near here—take samples and they will not match. They will be close but they will not match. You can go deep within the ocean, many fathoms, and it will be different. But in general, because of the livingness of things, and this is a concern of the Water Element. As long as there are plants and no pollution, the salt content will rise and will stay. But when the plants and the fish go, there is no livingness, pollution takes over and your earth must change.

For salt, or sodium is necessary in regards to the breathing aspect and the creation of what you might call the force areas, to allow the gravity to allow fresh air to stay within your earth cycle. Without the salt content in the seas, you would not have fresh air to breathe, it goes high, creates an Element that helps you to live—apart from the Living Spirit. Peace."

The Student continued,

"There is an aspect of free flow of which I would like to ask you. When you speak of spiritual evolution and free flow and how they go hand in hand, should we presume, not presume, but attempt to be at a stage of evolution before one begins to live within free flow or does evolution follow free flow?"

"They walk hand in hand. Both go through the door at the same time. They are a mutual evolution awareness. One does not go before the other. Peace."

She continued,

"There is a great effort made to fend souls off from the Earth plane. Is this right?"

"You mean in regards to not having children? Keeping population down?

Old Chinese will just say they are physical or evolution. This is not right of course for there are souls that want to come in at this time. Did you know that you could take every

181

personage in your world, every personage, put them in a city like you are living in now, that would be the size of Europe, and use the rest of the earth for cultivation? It would fit. It would work.

Over-population is not the problem. You can cut back and have no children at all, but if you do not stop polluting the three Elements, it will not help. It is not correct, but those who are involved in it, that is their evolution. Peace."

Jonathon then began,

"They cut down a great many trees."

"This will help Air. But it is best to plant them where they will best be, where there is more population, not where there is no population. You don't want all the spirits in the desert, you want them here, for if they are in the desert you will surely have a cataclysm for the imbalance will cause a switch. It is true, planting and caring for green things, the plants who live refurbish the air, but also the water must not be polluted so that the plants can live. Peace"

The Student then asked,

"You said that every one of us here could feasibly reincarnate out in this life and you mentioned something about a life of service. What constitutes a life of service anyway?"

"Service does not mean saying prayers daily, or going about looking fierce. Service means this—loving yourself because the Living Spirit is within you, respecting all living things and realising that the Living Spirit is in all things, all living things. This sounds simple, but it is hard. But it is also simple, so simple it is hard.

You can serve in any place that you are, for there is need in every area. Personages that are willing to follow these things, but you will say, "I will be like a tiger that has squares instead of stripes."

Not true. At first you may be, but then you will be looked upon as someone who is in tune. There is a state that you must go through of agitation but once you reach above it, personages who are around you will want to be in that area also. Usually the person who talks for others receives the most criticism because others cannot reach there, but they do not criticise, they do not judge. Peace."

The Student said,

"When you say respect all life because of the Living Spirit, then what attitude should we take in contact with rodents in our daily lives in which we feel at the least the necessity to exterminate?"

"Why?"

"I suppose for what we call hygiene."

"If you are in free flow, you have no disease of the body. A rodent could bite you four times and you would be healthy. By being in free flow, respecting all living things, you would have cleanliness, there would be balance. They are necessary. It is man that makes rodents carry disease. In reality they do not.

It is in regards to perception, for you can have them within your pagoda and by loving, they will not harm. If they take cheese or if they take whatever, you are in free flow, you do not miss it. But if you love, there will not be any disease, harm or physical harm. That is a consciousness, that is a universal law. Peace."

She asked,

"When you mentioned dimension long ago, did they all exist simultaneously in the same area?"

"Not in the same area – same time, but not within time. It is only in the physical that you have minutes and hours. Peace."

Jonathon said,

"Does the Sphinx have any spiritual importance?"

"Now or then?"

"Then and now."

"Then it did. It was a temple and there is an underground passage from it to the Great Pyramid. When that is found there will be documents found. There are a lot of things laying within it.

The initiate entered the Sphinx, went into the Great Pyramid, and there within a state of suspended animation died for three days, or in essence, the soul left, went into the spiritual world for initiation, returned to the body after three days and then went out and worked within the world in the highest spiritual evolution.

And so you see, this was a part of the initiation at that time. Not only within the Pyramid, but within the Pythagorean theory. And so what the Nazarene did was not so new. Peace."

The Student thought for some minutes and then said,

"You mentioned that if we lived through the next cataclysm, we could reincarnate out, or if we came back within 500 of the earth years, we could reincarnate out. If neither of these came to pass we would have to reincarnate back into this world?"

"Once or twice. Most of you are in your eighth cycle so the odds are pretty high if you have an average of only nine. Peace. But do not relax. Peace. It is those that relax that are on their twenty fourth."

She said,

> "You mentioned that an imbalance of spirits, for example, could cause a cataclysm. What other things could cause it?"

> *"That is the only thing. It is a renewal of Nature, imbalance of the Air, of the Water, and the Earth spirits. That is what causes cataclysm. Peace. Continue."*

> "It is strange, when I was very small I seemed to be fascinated by salamanders and I had strange dreams about meeting salamanders. What does that signify?"

> *"It signifies that you are Fire.*

> *Old Chinese will give you some insight in regards to roles that can deal with one another better, let us say in female/male relations. The best two or the two that can come together are Fire and Water. Now they are not in regards to feeling that they are lower or higher, but in regards to relationships. Fire and Water. Fire and Earth. Most important, Air and Earth. Earth and Earth. The rest are chaos. Two Water Elements and your house is flooded, two Air Elements and you cannot stand because of the wind. Two Fire Elements and you burn up. None of you within this garden need worry. You will not burn or blow or flood. Peace."*

Jonathon's mind was filled with questions but as Old Chinese sank into the pose that signalled the beginning of his concluding parable, he relaxed. Even if this was their last meeting with Old Chinese he was certain that this was just the beginning of a lifetime of learning.

"In Old China, as the Sage was teaching students, he said, "Nature is the key, for in the naturalness of man as the plum orchard, or as the water, it is in naturalness. For as you see and feel, as you understand by letting things grow and by basically, the fire which brings things forward, the water which refreshes it, the wind which transplants it and allows fertilisation and the earth that brings forward in beauty."

Man is this—Man is Fire, Water, Air and Earth. Man is winter, spring, summer and fall. Man is Nature.

And when man lives in Nature, man will understand the peace within them. For it is like eating a plum, the taste is juicy, it refurbishes your body, but fruit is only good if it continually grows, continually contributes—that is what you are—growing Nature. Always knowing by respecting it, helping it evolve, letting it evolve undisturbed. So will man evolve.

And the Sage said, "What are you standing on?" And the student said, "Just earth, nothing important." And the Sage said, "I will take away all earth except what you are standing on. Then what is it?" The student said, "Then I have nothing."

So where you stand is not the important place, it is where you live, through your Fire, through your love, through your Water, through your emotion, through your Air, through your spiritual mentality, through your Earth, through your physical knowledge of bringing peace through Nature.

May each of you go forward in the peace that surrounds you and may you know that your Element is the one best for this evolution.

Blessings and peace."

The boys looked at Old Chinese and felt joy and understanding tinged with an immense sadness to be leaving him and the beautiful garden, perhaps for the last time. When they looked to the Student she shrugged and looked towards the sky with tears welling in her eyes.

The boys left, as usual, in silence. Taylor felt unexpected dismay that their learning with Old Chinese seemed to be over. Jonathon experienced a subtle dread at the thought of having to make his own way in life now without the help of the old man. And at the same time both felt gratitude, knowing that the understandings they had gained would be invaluable to them in the coming times.

Jonathon had the sense that there might yet be one last meeting with Old Chinese but he did not want to say anything to Taylor in case his hunch was unfounded.

Chapter 20 – The Run

Jono burst in the door panting, having obviously run all the way home from the park. He looked at me, eyes sparkling.

"I think I can guess where you've been," I said.

He was standing in the dining room, breathing too heavily to do anything more than nod, but he was clearly wanting to talk.

Finally, he said,

"Dad, I think it's all kind of fitting into place now that we have heard the fourth Element. Do you think…?"

I stopped him.

"Jono, don't talk about it yet. I know you now have all the information around 'The Elements of Man' but there's still more to learn. And most importantly, the energy needs to integrate within you. I suggest you sleep on it before we talk about it and then it won't take long for you to put it all together.

Jonathon, remember my Ironman story? I haven't shared with you what happened on the run yet.

The run is certainly physical. From my first steps, the pounding put my shoulder into spasm and excruciating pain. It was relieved marginally when a kind volunteer at an aid station put a sling on my arm, which reduced the jolting effect of gravity. I struggled through that five and a half hour run in constant pain, but for some reason I continued, though I must admit, there were times when I did consider stopping. My mind created multiple reasons to stop, but something kept me going, overriding the messages from my brain—a kind of inner confidence that I would survive.

I finished the race in tears of joy and exhaustion—feeling totally triumphant.

One of my most powerful and precious memories from that race, Jono, is seeing you waiting to give me a high-five just before the finishing straight. I took off my sling just before I got to you and I will never forget the fear in your eyes when you saw the amount of strapping on my shoulder. You were only a child, but I also saw your admiration and relief as I passed you and your knowing that I would finish.

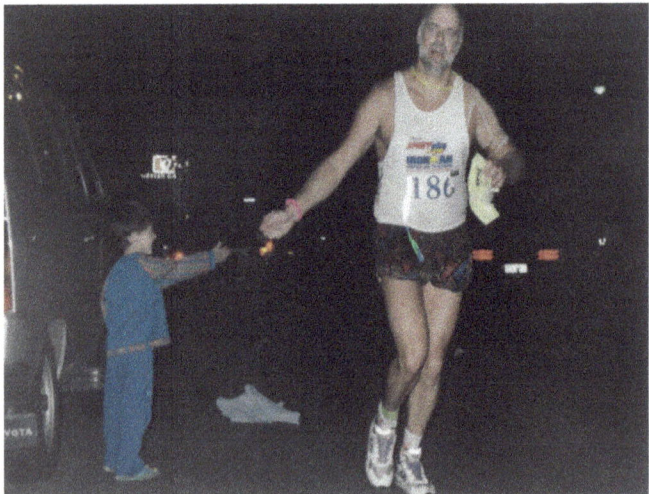

Jono, whenever I would complete a race, especially that one, the internal satisfaction was indescribable. Within a couple of days, the pain would ease and I'd feel a new level of understanding and connection to what drives me spiritually.

I've always tried to teach you to not fear the unknown. I guess doing triathlons was my way of doing that in my life. It's up to you to find the way that works best for you."

Jonathon silently nodded as he turned to go to his room.

Chapter 21 – The Gnomes

From the Earth teaching the boys already knew that the gnomes were the Earth Elementals and they wanted to meet them. For the rest of March they were vigilant during their time in the park. They revisited all the areas where they had previously encountered the Student, but without success. If they were to complete their learning they would need to find the Elemental spirit of autumn.

Finally they resorted to searching areas of the park they'd not explored together before. Some, Taylor recalled discovering as a child, but all were completely unknown to Jonathon.

Late one afternoon they ventured into the thick undergrowth along the northern boundary of the park. Jonathon was more than a little concerned, crawling through the dense foliage beneath a canopy of tall ferns. Suddenly, they heard the Student's voice. As they approached, she motioned for them to sit down and be quiet.

As Taylor sat down he felt a sharp pain in his rear end. He wriggled to one side and, without looking, felt for the source of the annoyance. His hand grasped a long, pointed stone, which, without thinking, he placed in his pocket.

Soon, to their absolute astonishment, they saw little people emerging from behind bushes and the dark mouth of a small cave set amongst ghostly boulders.

She whispered,

> "These are the gnomes of Nature. They are evolving through the physical Elements of Nature and are

Earth's spirits working in a vibration similar to the plants, animals, and minerals of the forest and caves.

There are many types of gnomes. For example, the pygmies work with stones, gems and metals and are the guardians of hidden treasures. Every shrub and flower has its own Nature spirit.

The gnomes are of various sizes, usually much smaller than human beings, though some are similar in size, whilst still others have the power to change their stature. When the gnomes are working with animals or humans their labour is confined to issues corresponding with their own natures. The Earth spirits meet at certain times of year in great enclaves as described by William Shakespeare in 'A Midsummer Night's Dream.'

Because the gnomes dwell in the darkness of caves and the gloom of forests, their temperament is melancholy and despondent. Often people think that the disposition of the gnomes is malicious and treacherous but this is not true, as they merely reflect the emotions of the humans and animals near them.

Gnomes are said to have incredible appetites and earn their food by diligent and conscientious labour. Most of them are of a miserly temperament and like storing things away in secret places. This is why small children often see them as their contact with the material side of Nature, and that is why children often hide things away.

The gnomes are the Elemental representation of autumn and of Earth Elements. The Earth Elements are the physical and material Elements of the Earth. Everything they must learn is related to the physical.

They are most content living in Nature."

The boys watched the gnomes for a considerable period as they collected plant food and carried it into the cave. It seemed that the small family groups delighted in working and playing deep in the gloomy forest.

As the boys left the forest that day, the sense of privilege they felt at having been given ancient understandings was tinged with sadness. They both knew that they may never again see the Student or the magical spirits that she had brought into their lives.

Chapter 22 – The Rugby Players

Taylor's motivation increased as they neared the completion of their quest. He knew it meant his reward was imminent. Both boys embarked on their search with renewed determination. But how would they go about finding a living example of the Earth or physical Element as described by Old Chinese? Jonathon suspected that they might look different to the other Elements.

They watched many people who came to various places in the park, feeling that they were now able to recognise a Fire Element, as distinct from the Water Elements and the solitary Air Elements. But the physical/material people continued to evade them.

Jonathon became irritated and frustrated and felt that his intuition was letting him down because he could not find them.

Late one afternoon the boys collapsed exhausted at the base of one of the giant elm trees in a corner of the park near the football oval. Beneath them lay a crackling carpet of fallen leaves that ranged in colour from green to yellow through red. The enormous trees and the ground surrounding them were ablaze with the shades of autumn.

As they sat with their backs resting against the trunk of their favourite tree both were lost in thought. Silently, a ruby red elm leaf fluttered down and landed on the toe of Jonathon's running shoe. As he kicked it away their peace was shattered by a group of six rugby players at one of the exercise stations that criss-crossed the running track through the park.

Taylor recognised the rugby players as members of the local first-grade team. The players dropped to the ground at the exercise station, grunted their way through about 20 push-ups, then rose and sprinted to the next exercise station where they launched into a series of sit-ups. A further group, similar in number, followed the first. Within about five minutes the entire team and reserves had passed by the boys as they looked down from their position on a small hill.

Jonathon said to Taylor,

> "Look at those muscles. That is definitely what you would call very physical... maybe..."

Rising in unison, they followed the players to the football oval. There the team milled around catching their breath and waiting for instructions for more drills. The boys recognised the coach as a teacher from their school. Sitting at the foot of the small grandstand they watched the players training.

Jonathon mused,

> "Some of them are tall and skinny, some small and more agile, but just take a look at those front rowers. Most of them look like they could lift a car. They are not particularly fast, but they look incredibly strong. I'm thinking that they could be the Earth or physical Elements that Old Chinese talked about."

Taylor said,

> "Well, they are rugby players so they have to be strong but you might be right. Most of them are dedicated to their game and that means they have to be into strength and fitness."

After training, Taylor approached Brian Jones, who had just left High School the year before. Brian was hooker in the team. Whilst Taylor chatted to him Jonathon noted that Brian appeared to be a ball of muscle with incredibly strong shoulders and almost no neck. Afterwards Jonathon watched as Brian drove off in his father's Mustang 'muscle' car.

Some of these rugby players, especially the front rowers, who appeared so physical, seemed to fit Old Chinese's description of Earth. Jonathon felt elated at the thought that they may have found the final Element described by Old Chinese.

Their excitement was somewhat tempered, however, by the realisation that their time with Old Chinese and their quest might now be finishing.

Chapter 23 – The Questions

It was late and Jonathon was unable to fall asleep. He reflected on the Elements, the Elementals and the people that they had studied in the park. He still had many questions. What was the meaning of the Elementals in the present day? What did this all mean for him personally and how was he to use it in his life?

Jonathon felt more and more frustrated by the myriad thoughts rampaging in his head. It seemed that the more he sought clarity, the harder it was to work out what it all meant. He longed to approach his father to discuss all that had happened, but knew he couldn't—not without breaching the confidence of Old Chinese.

One thing in particular stuck in his mind as he attempted to reconcile all he had learned. In the last parable Old Chinese had said that man is Fire, Water, Air and Earth, just like Nature. He said that man is winter, spring, summer and autumn. Man is Nature.

Agonising over his thoughts, Jonathon finally drifted off. Almost immediately he sensed a presence in the room, yet was uncertain whether he was awake or dreaming. The figure appeared to be his father and they were in Don's Room of Mysteries. The father figure leaned towards Jonathon nonchalantly, with one elbow against the altar, and looked directly at him.

The father figure said,

> "Jonathon, you are asking the wrong questions. Ask instead what you have learned about yourself? Stop thinking this to death—thoughts are like air and just like the sylph, they are elusive. You cannot grab onto

the air. Seek your answers within, not without and you will find peace."

Jonathon sat bolt upright in bed. The dream had impacted him deeply. Was this the answer to his question? Could it be that he was an Air Element? If so, he now knew that his lesson in life was to stop intellectualising, to stop thinking things to death.

He then had a flashback of being in Taylor's messy bedroom and the way he had judged Taylor for not being able to keep his room tidy. Was this response yet another piece of the jigsaw? He suspected that judgement was an Air response.

Next, he was filled with sadness as he saw the judgements he'd been holding around his father for taking him away from all of his friends and bringing him to New Zealand.

Everything he'd learned seemed to be coming together. He recognised himself as an Air Element, knew with absolute clarity that summer was his season and that his lesson in life was to stop using his intellect to judge others. Jonathon realised that the essence of Old Chinese's teaching was that to be in a balance, each Element must deal with their primary life lesson. That lesson lay in integrating the other three Elements. But how could he do that? He thought about it for days, at the same time aware that he was still thinking things to death.

One night, as Jonathon drifted off to sleep, he thought of Taylor. He knew that his friend would also need to understand his personal life lesson. Jonathon resolved to at least help him discover the right questions.

In the morning however, he wasn't sure he still remembered all of the pieces of the puzzle. Dismayed, he decided that he needed to talk to Taylor. He knew he couldn't yet talk to his father though he now understood that he was watching over him—as was The Elements of Man. But he felt the need to discuss the teachings with someone who had just been through it.

He also hoped there would be an opportunity to verify his new learning—perhaps with Old Chinese?

Chapter 24 – An Answer

After school Jonathon walked to Taylor's house. This time he made a conscious effort to remain neutral as he picked his way through the mess on Taylor's floor.

He sat down on Taylor's bed and said,

"I think I may have worked it out."

Taylor said,

"What? You mean about the Elements?"

"Yep. Look, we know that the Fire Elements need to learn to love themselves, Water Elements need to balance emotion, and Air Elements need to get out of their heads. But what about Earth?"

Jonathon glanced at Taylor before continuing.

"Plus, I've been trying to figure out where we fit in ...?"

Taylor had a weird expression on his face and he interrupted,

"Do you remember when we saw the gnomes? I couldn't tell you before, but I found something while we were sitting in the forest. I thought it was just a rock but when I washed it, it looked interesting, so I took it over to show Don. Turns out, it's quartz crystal."

"But what's that got to do with us and Old Chinese?" said Jonathon.

"Clear quartz crystal is made of silica which Don reckons isn't found around here. We have no idea how it came to be in the park."

Taylor continued,

"He says that crystals have memory and if you program something into a crystal it remembers that vibration forever until it's erased. Don told me that the Egyptians guarded the tombs of the Pharaohs with crystals that had been programmed or encoded with a particular vibrational energy and that crystals were used in Atlantis to control the people."

This was all new to Jonathon. He said,

"I knew that digital watches and computers all use quartz or silica, but how do you program a crystal?"

"Here," said Taylor handing a book to Jonathon.

"Don gave me this book and it's all explained in here. The author, Frank Dorland, was an expert on crystals who lived in California. Have you ever heard of the Crystal Skulls?

Jonathon's eyes widened in response to the question.

"Apparently there were once about 12 life-size crystal skulls and some of them have been found in various parts of Central America. Frank Dorland spent years examining one that this explorer, Mitchell-Hedges, claimed his daughter found in ancient Mayan or Aztec ruins. It was even named after him but other researchers think he bought it in London in 1943."

"What were the skulls used for?" asked Jonathon, staring at a page showing a picture of the Mitchell-Hedges skull.

"According to the book they were ancient talismans used by shamans to control their people. They used to put a flame under the skull so that light shone out through the eyes—pretty spooky! Don reckons they are repositories of ancient wisdom, and if we know how to decode them they might hold a record of their times, a bit like we use computers and CD-Roms to store information now. Apparently they took centuries to shape and polish because they were all carved by hand."

Taylor could sense Jonathon's mind trying to piece together the relevance of all this stuff about crystals just as he had when Don had first shared this information with him.

He held the clear quartz crystal up so Jonathon could see. It was hexagonal in shape about two inches long and its six facets merged into a point on top. A slight movement allowed it to catch the light creating a rainbow of colours dancing on his bedroom wall.

Taylor recounted that after reading the book he had lain in bed several nights wondering whether the crystal he'd found contained some special meaning or message for him. He recalled how Old Chinese had said that there are four kingdoms and that Fire was in charge of Man, Water was in charge of animal, Air was in charge of plant and Earth in charge of mineral.

He'd dreamed about the gnomes, working with the plants, animals and minerals in the forest. In his dream the gnomes had given him the crystal and shown him how to 'program' it for a particular purpose.

The dream had stayed with him so he used the words he was shown in the dream to program his crystal. One thing he'd learned from Don was not to tell anyone what you dedicate your crystal to or it loses its power. It was several days later when it struck him that perhaps the crystal was another clue about his Element? He did, after all, relate to the physicality of Earth more than any of the other Elements. He was more muscular than Jonathon and he seemed to have a special relationship with the park and the gnomes.

Finally Taylor looked squarely at Jonathon and announced,

"I reckon I'm an Earth Element."

He paused, dropping his gaze. After some moments he said,

"But if I am Earth, I'm not so sure that I've figured out my Elemental life lesson."

Jonathon gave him a quizzical look as he realised in that instant that Taylor's admission of this *was* his lesson...or at least a good part of it.

Taylor continued,

"I have to work it out before I get my reward, don't I?"

There was a long pause.

"I know I've been giving you a hard time about getting my reward...and well, Jono, I'm sorry...I sort of get it now. Understanding the Elements is a bit like figuring out the clues on one of Don's puzzles but what I didn't get until just now is that each of us *is* the answer.

It's pretty useless having the key if you don't know where the treasure is, though. I see now that it's not about knowing anyone else's Element—all I have to do is know my own and understand myself. That's the quest—that's what Don's been trying to teach me!"

With Taylor's admission it felt like weeks of accumulated tension between them just melted away and they smiled knowingly at each other.

Jonathon stood to leave, turned back to Taylor and then sat down again.

Taylor looked at him and said,

"What?"

Jonathon squirmed a little on the bed and said,

"What about the project?"

Taylor immediately retorted,

"What about it?"

Jonathon thought for a few moments before replying.

"Taylor, it never was a school project. We can't hand it in at school."

"Why?"

Jonathon chose his words carefully.

> "Well, we have all this information and sketches but who is going to understand it? The teacher and the class haven't heard what Old Chinese has said and no one will know what we are on about. We can't teach them the 'Elements of Man'."

Taylor thought for a moment and then said,

> "But what about all of our work?"

Jonathon rose to his feet, turned towards the door and said over his shoulder,

> "It's our lesson."

Jonathon left, relieved that Taylor had managed to work his Element out for himself and that he was beginning to ask the right questions. He was intrigued that they had been having parallel experiences concerning their Elemental lessons and felt certain that they had now arrived at the place they both needed to be in order for the next step to unfold.

He wondered if this experience contained yet another lesson—that neither of them could progress and attain their ultimate reward without the other. He felt that their reward would only come about as a result of his support for Taylor.

He thought back over the resistance he'd encountered from Taylor throughout the time they'd worked on their project and now saw that it was part of the journey. He also thought about Taylor's concern about telling Don of the robbery. He simply did not know an answer to this question, however some inner voice was saying to him,

"It's not your problem. Do not get involved."

Taylor and him together—they had both the map and the key. He realised that it's the same in life. You can only grow and be successful through helping others to grow and succeed. Perhaps that's what Old Chinese had meant about needing to integrate the lessons of all of the Elements.

Their research was now complete. Or was it really over? He remembered that Old Chinese had said that most people are a combination of two Elements. And his father seemed to be saying that the Elements represented a life-long process. It felt to Jonathon that the learning was only just beginning.

The one burning question that still plagued Jonathon, however, was who or what might be behind all of this orchestrating the events that appeared to be leading up to 'the promise'?

Chapter 25 – The Elements of Man Revealed

Taylor felt confused. He was now quite close to Don and felt an obligation to tell him about the robbery. On the other hand, after many months of thinking about Old Chinese's words he felt that he should not interfere. Old Chinese wanted to teach him that being robbed or any other accident is not an accident at all but is brought about, somehow, by the person himself. He understood the words but he still wanted to be honest with Don. He also knew that he could not talk directly to Don about what Old Chinese had taught them.

He could not get the scene of the robbery out of his mind and one day in the Room of Mysteries, feeling distinctly guilty he said to Don,

"You know how your shop got robbed last year?"

Don studied him for a moment and then responded,

"Taylor don't worry about that. It was my fault. I didn't lock up properly."

Taylor was dumbfounded. He tried to conceal his amazement at Don's words and went on playing with the puzzle in his hands. He instantly felt a huge rush of relief and knew in that instant that Old Chinese was right.

Jonathon knew that Taylor expected him to deliver on the promised 'experience'. But he also knew he couldn't reveal anything about it. He agonised for days about how to make it happen. Meanwhile, Taylor continued to demand his reward. Jonathon was trapped between Old Chinese's request for secrecy and his commitment to show Taylor what he had seen. Unable to resolve his dilemma he went to see Don Adkins one morning on his way to school.

Explaining his problem to Don in the most general of terms, Don suggested capturing Taylor's interest by tapping into his newfound interest.

"Why don't we make a puzzle for him to solve? The right questions could lead him to the answer."

Jonathon thought for a moment and said,

"I don't know what the initial clues might be but here's the answer he must arrive at."

He reached into his pocket, scribbled on a fragment of paper, folded it and then handed it to Don.

Don glanced at the tattered paper and nodded knowingly,

"Easy! Leave it to me. I'll set up a puzzle he can't resist."

To Jonathon's relief, Don didn't ask him anything further. If anyone could be relied on to understand a mystery or keep a secret, Don could.

One week later, on the eve of the full moon, Jonathon stood alone amongst the dense foliage above the waterfall. He was freezing and desperately hoping that Taylor had found the clues that would lead him here.

As time wore on, doubts began to gnaw at him and he wondered if he had the right night. What if he ended up standing here alone all night? He would feel pretty foolish.

He recalled a conversation he'd had with his father the

night before. In it Jonathon had said,

> "Dad now that we have learned of The Elements of Man, what Element am I? What Element are you?"

Slowly his father had responded,

> "Jono, it is really for you to allow the energy to settle within you. In time the Elements will become clear to you. Your own may take longer to work out than the Elements of other people."

Jonathon replied,

> "Dad, we have picked up hints about face and body shapes from our project. I think Air Elements have an oval face."

Knowing that he was trying to rationalise an enormous amount of knowledge Jonathon recalled his father also saying,

> "Jono, Old Chinese has probably told you that most people are a combination of two Elements. If you look at my oval face, my long legs and my occupation based around thinking you might guess that I am an Air Element. But I am also touched by Earth and so have strong muscle development and physical competence. That is what helped me to get through the Ironman Triathlons. So I am a combination of Air and Earth. Do not over-think it. It will become crystal clear to you along the way."

The last words brought him back to reality. The conversation faded away as he returned to his dark and lonely place in the park.

The voices of doubt and indecision grew louder, almost mocking and a million questions flooded his brain. Is it the right night? Will Old Chinese or the Student be here? When will they appear? Would Old Chinese show them the wonders he had foreshadowed when they'd met so long ago? The only thing he could be certain of was that a voice inside him kept saying, "This is the day."

Now sitting on the cold ground, almost dozing off, the sound of a breaking twig interrupted his thoughts. He twisted around to see Taylor picking his way through the bushes toward him. Jonathon scrambled to his feet.

Behind Taylor, further down the path, Jonathon caught a fleeting glimpse of a tall ghostly figure. He strained to see more clearly but by then it was gone.

In the light of the full moon Taylor looked enquiringly into Jonathon's eyes. Neither said a word. The boys stood close together on the small rocky outcrop above the waterfall watching it splash freezing water onto the rocks below. This was near to where they had learned of the energy of the undine.

It was cold and dark. Taylor had no idea what, if anything, was about to happen. He looked at his friend. Jonathon appeared equally uncertain.

Through the mists drifting up from the base of the waterfall, the Student silently appeared beside them.

"Come with me," she said.

Jonathon gulped audibly still wondering whether he would be able to deliver on his promise to Taylor.

She turned and confidently pulled aside the branches of a large bush revealing a stone pathway plunging into the darkness at the base of the waterfall. As they descended the slippery path in silence, Taylor, cold and a little frightened, glanced nervously in every direction. Jonathon made an effort to appear composed but his legs felt like they might give way at any moment and he grasped at bushes and rocks to steady himself.

At the bottom they were greeted by the gaping blackness of a cave whose entrance lay beneath the waterfall. It was concealed from above and was invisible from the duck pond.

To Taylor's complete shock and Jonathon's immense relief, shrouded in mist and sitting on the wet rocks outside the cave entrance was Old Chinese. Seated silently at his feet were one of each of the Elementals—a salamander, an undine, a sylph and a gnome. All were peering into the darkness of the cave.

"Sit with me at his feet and say nothing," the Student commanded in whispered tones.

Jonathon's trepidation now gave way to euphoria at being close to Old Chinese and the Elementals once again. He peered through the mist at the cave entrance. The cave seemed to exude a certain energy and, although Jonathon had felt it before, the hairs on the back of his neck stood to attention. Taylor sat silently on the wet rock feeling a mixture of fear and anticipation as the all-enveloping mist left a shimmering coating of moisture on his face and hands.

Over the gentle rumble of falling water, they became aware of a rhythmic humming coming from behind the waterfall. Through the swirling mist the boys sensed, rather than saw, the silhouettes of heavily shrouded figures moving in a luminescent glow at the mouth of the cave. Tiny flashes of light shot through the darkness like lightning, dancing about the heads of several of the figures.

Jonathon continued to stare at the ghostly figures. Some were larger than others, some had indistinct faces, whilst others looked to have almost human form beneath their long dark hooded robes. Here was a host of mysterious figures apparently focusing their attention on those outside the cave.

Jonathon sensed a different energy emanating from each figure. They said nothing audible but Jonathon knew that they were The Brotherhood and that they numbered 33. Each figure was a repository of knowledge and information, and each had its own story to tell. And there—just one amongst many—stood 'The Elements of Man'.

As the figure stepped forward Jonathon knew it was a different figure to the one he had previously seem. He was initially scared as it focused its attention directly on him but he somehow knew that the figure was there to support him. The figure wordlessly confirmed to him what he had learned of 'The Elements of Man'.

Jonathon glanced at Taylor. In the mist-laden atmosphere Jonathon thought he could make out a tear rolling down Taylor's cheek. Taylor turned to him and smiled. In that moment Jonathon felt that their teaching was complete. Then his attention was drawn to the other 32. As he stared at them he realized that this was just the beginning.

In the presence of Old Chinese, the Student, the Elementals and now these all-knowing figures, Jonathon felt humbled. Why had he been chosen to receive these ancient and mystical understandings?

He did not know why. What he did know was that he was now on a lifetime journey that required him to appreciate and evolve these ancient understandings.

The Student then stood, bowed to Old Chinese and quietly led the two boys up the tortuous path through the mist-laden atmosphere. They all climbed in silence each struggling with the energy of what they had seen and felt. At the top she saw them past the bushes then turned and re-traced her steps.

After she had disappeared and the branches had closed, Jonathon felt totally alone even though Taylor was but a few feet away. After staring forlornly at the bushes he turned to face Taylor. As he spun around he came face to face with a frightening dark, towering figure. He was too shocked to scream but stumbled back in fear.

He searched for a face as his eyes tried to focus. The incandescent glow of the moon framed the face from behind but he could not make out any features. As his gaze drifted lower he was shocked to see that its clothes sparkled with droplets of water—just like his and Taylor's.

Still reeling from the unexpected presence of another person—one who had obviously been at the base of the waterfall—Jonathon's mind raced.

Again Jonathon was tempted to run but for some reason he hesitated. Then the figure slowly reached out toward him. As it did Jonathon closed his eyes. He felt his body stiffen as he held his breath.

He waited.

Then he felt wet clothing touch his shoulder. He shuddered and involuntarily opened his eyes. As he did so he felt the figure put its arm around his shoulders.

As he flinched, he heard a comforting voice—his father's—say,

"Come on Jono, let's go home."

Epilogue

And so it has come full circle.

The journey that I started so many years ago led me to the wonders of metaphysics and 'The Elements of Man' and to the mysteries of the park. These and other experiences remain alive in my mind and spirit.

As for Jonathon, he has learned a great deal about the 'Elements of Man' however he does not yet appreciate how much more there is to learn and how that knowledge will imbue his life with joy.

At some point in his life, I am certain he will appreciate the energy and wisdom that will be brought into his life by the remaining 32 energies of The Brotherhood.

And it truly is just the beginning—the beginning of a journey that will continue for the rest of our lives.

I am proud that I have been able to offer Jonathon and Taylor the opportunity of commencing their journey whilst still in their teens.

In the time it had taken them to experience each season they had entered the first cycle of a journey. A journey that will take them—as long as it takes.

References

Manly P. Hall   The Secret Teachings of All Ages

Acknowledgments

Project Consultant/Editor: Jennifer Moalem

Edits/Proofing: Leigh Robshaw

Technical Advice and Design: Judy MacGraw

Graphic Design   Purple Munkey

Copywriting   Heather Zahar

Typing: Saada Iskandar

Illustrations: Geraldine Gallagher

Photographs: The Author and by kind courtesy of *Invercargill City Council* and *Venture Southland*

www.ingramcontent.com/pod-product-compliance
Lightning Source LLC
Chambersburg PA
CBHW041255040426
42334CB00028BA/3031